Ecocity
Snapshots
Learning from Europe's Greenest Places

RICK PRUETZ

Also by Rick Pruetz

The TDR Handbook: Designing and Implementing Transfer of Development Rights Programs

(co-author with Arthur C. Nelson and Doug Woodruff

Lasting Value: Open Space Planning and Preservation Successes

Beyond Takings and Givings: Saving Natural Areas, Farmland and Historic Landmarks

with Transfer of Development Rights and Density Transfer Charges

Saved By Development: Preserving Environmental Areas, Farmland and Historic Landmarks

with Transfer of Development Rights

Putting Transfer of Development Rights to Work in California

Arje Press
ISBN-13: 978-0692794654

DEDICATION

To Adrian, Jay, Erica, Gena, Jeromy, Josh, Kayla, Cate and the memory of my parents, Eric and Jean

CONTENTS

List of Illustrations

Preface

As this book's title suggests, the profiles of 19 European cities found here are like snapshots, impressions that depict only a fraction of the scope and depth of our difficult but essential path toward sustainability. Despite their limitations, I hope these snapshots help inspire readers to join or at least learn more about the ecocity movement. Maybe they will simply help you convince skeptics, and perhaps yourself, that remarkable progress is possible when you pursue ambitious goals.

As further explained in the Acknowledgements section, this book springs from my involvement with Ecocity Builders, a non-profit organization promoting the emergence of cities in balance with nature. Over many years, Richard Register, founder of Ecocity Builders, and Kirstin Miller, Executive Director, have asked me to speak at meetings and conferences about transferable development rights, a planning tool that uses development to pay for various community benefits, including the preservation of natural areas, farmland and historic landmarks. Then I agreed to join the Ecocity Builders Board of Directors.

Ecocity Builders' largest project at the moment is UrbInsight, a participatory mapping and planning process used in Cairo, Egypt, Casablanca, Morocco, Cusco, Peru and Medellin, Columbia to date. But Ecocity Builders is also the keeper of the Ecocity World Summit, launched in 1990, held in cities all over the planet and now the longest-running international ecocity conference series.

Nantes, France hosted our 2013 Ecocity World Summit. Not coincidentally, we were there when this fun-loving city was celebrating its reign as the 2013 European Green Capital. Most memorably, this collaboration climaxed at a dinner for 5,000 people held in Nantes' repurposed shipyards where we enjoyed a tasty meal made from vegetables considered too ugly to be sold in food stores.

Traveling to the 2013 Ecocity World Summit also gave me the opportunity to visit four other cities that had been named European Green Capitals, the award granted each year by the European Commission to one city demonstrating exemplary progress toward sustainability. To sample the green networks of these cities, I biked the Alsterwanderweg trail from downtown Hamburg, Germany to the wooded nature reserves ringing that city. I rode the bike paths that completely encircle Vitoria-Gasteiz, Spain within a greenbelt created largely from restored wetlands, landfills and gravel pits. I tested the eco-mobility of Copenhagen and was heartened to discover that the model ecodistrict of Hammarby Sjostad in Stockholm is a pleasant neighborhood while also doubling as a living laboratory for closed-loop systems. By the end of that trip, I wanted to explore more of these planet-friendly role models.

The Tomorrow's Cities Today conference held in London in June 2015 and our Ecocity World Summit held in Abu Dhabi in October 2015 gave me two more great excuses to visit 14 additional cities which have either won the European Green Capitals competition or have received other recognition including shortlisting as a European Green Capital or winning the European Green Leaf, the award recently launched by the European Commission for cities with populations ranging from 20,000 to 100,000.

In assembling each profile for this book, I used any information I could find in English from and about these cities. In particular, I relied heavily on the European Commission's many publications including applications for the awards, expert panel evaluations and reports highlighting the best practices generated by the 126 entries received in the eight years since the rollout of the European Green Capitals program in 2008. These programs have been invaluable in helping me identify and describe some of Europe's most ambitious cities. However, as I mention in Chapter One, the European Green Capitals competition does not attempt to rate the entire spectrum of sustainability.

In contrast, the Ecocity Framework developed by Ecocity Builders and the British Columbia Institute of Technology (BCIT) aims to evaluate cities for culture, well-being, education, economy, governance and food systems as well as attributes used in the European Green Capitals' approach such as mobility, biodiversity, air, land, water and energy. Significantly, the Ecocity Framework also assesses whether a city is living within the planet's carrying capacity or consuming more than its fair share of Earth's resources. As of August 2016, a team of expert advisors led by Jennie Moore, Associate Dean of BCIT's School of Construction and the Environment, continues to develop indicators with the goal of making the Ecocity Framework a more holistic approach to comprehensively assessing progress toward true sustainability. But for now, we can still admire, envy, be inspired by and learn from Europe's greenest places.

CHAPTER 1

Europe's Greenest Places

Cities are key to our planet's future. Over half of us now live in cities and an estimated 70 percent of the world's total population will be urban by 2050 -- over six billion people. Will tomorrow's cities continue to waste land, squander resources and contaminate water and air in an escalation of our centuries-old war on the Earth? Or will we build and rebuild cities that return us to a balance with nature in ways that are mutually beneficial to people and our fellow creatures?

Europe's greenest places offer hope for a positive outcome. The 19 cities profiled in this book are reintroducing greenways and stream corridors into the urban landscape, often in ways that assist with floodwater management and biodiversity while reconnecting people with their environment. These cities are building compact, diverse neighborhoods that can easily be navigated on foot or by bicycle and public transportation. They are turning brownfields into ecodistricts that expand the limits of closed-loop energy, waste and water systems. They are cutting the greenhouse gas emissions that cause climate change and pursuing a carbon-free future by fueling district heating and power systems using wind, water, geothermal, biomass and other innovative technologies. Recognizing that individual behavior is crucial to sustainability, these cities motivate their citizens to understand the connection between their lifestyles and the health of the planet. Ironically, while naysayers claim that sustainability is unattainable or unaffordable, these cities are finding that green is good for economic development, generating businesses and jobs in rapidly-growing sectors and attracting the highly-prized creative class with their mix of vibrant urbanity and accessible nature.

What are Ecocities?

Ecocities are communities in balance with nature. But how can we measure a city's balance with nature? Dozens of ecocity evaluation approaches have been proposed (Joss, 2012). But no single method has yet been chosen due to the vast differences in cities and the time needed to evaluate each approach (Joss, 2015). This book largely uses the evaluation criteria developed by the European Commission for the European Green Capitals award competition and the European Greenleaf contest available to smaller cities. Cities in these competitions are judged by their accomplishments in twelve environmental indicators: climate action, transportation, greenspace/land use, biodiversity, air quality, noise, eco-innovation, energy performance, integrated environmental planning and management of water, waste and wastewater. The European Green Capitals program also recognizes strategies that motivate citizens to lead more sustainable lives since physical improvements are futile unless accompanied by changes in human behavior.

The European Green Capitals evaluation process is arguably the best currently- available framework for exploring Europe's green places. But, it does not fully address all aspects of a city's balance with nature. For example, the European Commission does not ask applicant cities to estimate their total ecological footprint. A true ecocity would ideally be a one-planet city: it would maintain a level of consumption that Earth could support even if every city in the world consumed resources at that level. In reality, experts believe that three planets would be needed if everyone on Earth had ecological footprints comparable to typical European cities including cities in Sweden, Norway, Spain, Germany and the United Kingdom (Moore, 2015). While the 19 cities profiled in this book are making

Figure 1-1: *Heidelberg is surrounded by the 3,500 square kilometer UNESCO Geo-Naturepark Bergstrasse-Odenwald.*

commendable progress considering their affluence, the European GreenCapitals competition does not ask if their total consumption levels are getting closer to those of the one-planet-city-levels met and even exceeded by many poverty-stricken cities typically found in Asia, Africa and Latin America (Moore and Rees, 2013).

That said, success in the European Green Capitals or European Greenleaf competitions shows that a city is making remarkable progress toward sustainability even though that city may not yet be in complete balance with nature. Consequently, the 19 cities profiled in this book are clearly role models when judged according to the criteria established by the European Commission. In fact, 15 of these cities have either won this award or been named as finalists in the European Green Capital and European Greenleaf award programs.

The twelve environmental indicators in the European Green Capitals program create a comprehensive evaluation process and all twelve are discussed in the city profiles found in later chapters. But to emphasize important distinctions and avoid repetition, this chapter introduces key concepts and examples from the case studies using nine categories: greenspace and green networks; compact, mixed use neighborhoods; pedestrian friendliness; bicycle infrastructure and public transportation; nature and biodiversity; redevelopment of brownfields into ecodistricts; climate action and alternative energy; public engagement; and economic development through sustainability.

Green Structure

Sustainable cities centralize growth while maintaining and often increasing parkland, habitat and other greenspace. Furthermore, these cities put people and nature close together. In most of the cities profiled in this book, the vast majority of residents live within 300 meters of green space. In some, like Vitoria-Gasteiz, Spain, Ljubljana, Slovenia, and Essen, Germany, almost everyone lives within 300 meters of some kind of green area.

However, sustainable cities are not content to simply locate large amounts of greenspace close to people. These cities also strive to connect greenspace in ways that create a synergy for people, wildlife and community resilience. Green structures, (also referred to as green networks, green systems and green frameworks by the cities profiled in this book), often feature green corridors, or green fingers, that extend radially from the city center to preserved rural greenbelts surrounding compact urbanized areas. These green corridors are sometimes linked by concentric green rings that allow hikers, bicyclists and wildlife to move between greenways with minimal contact with cars and other manmade hazards. Some of green network plans envision a city in which people can use greenways to access schools, community centers, shopping and other daily needs under their own power, creating health benefits as well as recreation and environment-friendly transportation. By locating greenways within floodplains and other logical places, these cities create a green infrastructure that can protect water sources, defend against flash flooding and allow the reintroduction of plant and animal species that previous generations banished. As detailed below, the green structure concept particularly informs the planning and growth of Hamburg, Munster, Ljubljana, Copenhagen, Oslo, Helsinki, Stockholm, Nantes, Freiburg, Vitoria-Gasteiz and Essen.

The best time to plan a green structure was a century ago. And that is exactly what happened in some of these cities. Over 100 years ago, the Chief Building Officer of Hamburg, Germany proposed a web-like Grunesnetz featuring greenways radiating from the city center to the farms and woods of a rural greenbelt. In this plan, the spokes were connected by inner and outer green rings allowing non-motorized transportation throughout the city as well as recreational routes between the parks and, furthermore, between these parks and the surrounding countryside. The inner green ring was formed when the historic city walls were replaced by a string of parks and the Planten un Blomen botanical garden. From this inner ring, hikers and bicyclists can now follow the car-free Alsterwanderweg trail along the Alster River from downtown Hamburg to nature preserves in the city's hinterlands. Although incomplete, Hamburg is committed to protecting the Green Network as it currently exists and closing its remaining gaps (Hamburg, undated; European Commission, 2011).

Figure 1-2: *Hikers, bicyclists and even paddlers can meander the Alster River greenway from downtown Hamburg to the surrounding greenbelt.*

Munster, Germany transformed its former city walls into a walking and bicycling promenade that completely encircles the historic downtown. This green ring and two others connect seven green wedges extending into the Munsterland park landscape, a 6,000-square kilometer district protecting cultural landmarks as well as working farmland and wildlife habitat. One green wedge flanks a modest stream meandering across the city center and grows into a large linear park with a lake, museums and the city zoo (Munster, 2009; Munster, 2016).

Ljubljana, Slovenia created its inner green ring by transforming the strip of land that surrounded the city during World War II when a barbed wire fence separated the urban area from the surrounding countryside. Following liberation in 1945, the city converted this no-mans-land into the Path of Remembrance and Comradeship, a 33-kilometer walking-bicycling trail lined with 7,400 trees. Today, the Path is the site of a memorial walk held every year on the anniversary of the liberation. But year-round, Ljubljana residents use this path to exercise in natural surroundings and to reach many of the city's most popular parks and other destinations without a car (Valentine, 2010).

A 1928 vision for the Copenhagen region concentrated development within the central city and along radial urban corridors resembling fingers separated by rural land called green wedges. Although generally accepted, this concept had little official authority throughout the 20th century. Planners realized that the wedges were particularly vulnerable to sprawl unless they could be transformed into places that the general public would come to love and defend. Over the following nine decades, Copenhagen and surrounding municipalities created parks, forests, athletic fields, community gardens, golf courses and landscape protection areas. Through these efforts, average citizens likely realized the value of these areas and the green wedges were formally adopted by the Denmark Planning Act of 2007 (Copenhagen, 2011; Veire, Petersen and Henchel, undated).

The first parks plan of Oslo, Norway, adopted in 1917, envisioned green fingers along several streams linking the Oslo fiord with the Marka, the forested greenbelt that occupies two-thirds of the city's total land area. Subsequent plans built on that concept: higher density development within centers connected by trails linking schools, sporting fields, community facilities and open space including the surrounding Marka. Economic downturns and war slowed implementation. But Oslo has succeeded in creating a world-class green finger in Akerselva Environmental Park, which restores much of the Akerselva River to a near-natural state while converting many of the monumental factory buildings from Oslo's water-powered industrial era into restaurants, studios, entertainment venues, offices and housing. Energetic hikers and cyclists can use the trail system along the Akerselva to reach the Marka. But Oslo also offers a subway line from downtown that carries nature-seekers directly to trailheads in the greenbelt (Jorgensen and Kine, 2012).

In 1914, Helsinki, Finland, adopted a green structure plan linking local parks and public facilities with green fingers radiating from the downtown waterfront to farms and forests surrounding the city. Helsinki's 2050 City Plan repeats these goals, noting that increased density heightens the need for a green network that seamlessly connects parks, nature preserves, recreational centers, schools, shopping districts and workplaces. As a textbook example of a green finger, Central Park joins four nature protection areas north of the city with downtown Helsinki, where Cultural Park is home to several public facilities including the Opera House, the botanical garden and the Helsinki Music Center. Apparently pleased with the green structure concept, in 2002 the City Planning Department announced the creation of a highly-ambitious green finger called Helsinki Park incorporating rivers, coves, bays and islands in the Baltic Sea, including the historic Suomenlinna Island Fortress, a UNESCO World Heritage Site (Helsinki, 2013; Helsinki, 2015a; Helsinki, 2015b; Jaakkola, 2012).

Stockholm, Sweden essentially realized that it had created a green structure by concentrating development near its metro system and leaving the areas in between alone. In the 1990s, the Stockholm Regional Planning Office emphasized that these remnant green wedges were important to biodiversity as well as outdoor recreation and other environmental benefits. Today, the green wedges are designated in the regional plan as well as the plans of the region's 26 separate jurisdictions. From 20 to 30 percent of these green wedges are protected in eight nature reserves and the 2010 regional plan calls for additional preservation in its "never far from nature" vision. Many of these green wedges extend into the city center, including National City Park, said to be the world's first national urban park and home to four royal palaces as well as rare plant and animal species (Akerlund, 2011; European Commission, 2010; Floater, Rode and Zenghelis, 2013; Lantz, 2001; Lekberg, 2010; Nelson, undated; Office of Regional Planning, 2010).

Figure 1-3: *Vitoria's agricultural belt occupies 58 percent of the city's total land area.*

Nantes, France uses its network of over 250 kilometers of rivers and streams plus 9,500 hectares of wetlands to form its "green and blue framework". The banks of two of these rivers, the Loire and the Sevre, are Natura 2000 sites, a designation applied to almost 13 percent of the city's total land area. Nantes and the 23 surrounding communities are working together to restore aquatic ecosystems and revitalize habitat. In addition, Nantes offers 210 kilometers of "waterside walks" that provide "multimodal green transport" while connecting people with nature (European Commission, 2016; Nantes, 2010; O'Neill & Rudden, 2010).

In 1997, Freiburg, Germany secured the western portion of its greenbelt by protecting 44 square miles of its lowland forest, or Mooswald, in a landscape conservation area that now provides a home for rare species of beetles, bats and woodpeckers as well as recreation for birders and nature lovers. The rest of the greenbelt is formed by the Black Forest, Schauinsland Mountain, the Rieselfeld nature reserve and the vineyards of Tuniberg as well as smaller greenspaces like Seepark, created for a 1986 garden expo, and Mundenhof, Freiburg's wildlife and nature park. Freiburg citizens and tourists can easily escape to nature by crossing a pedestrian bridge from downtown and wandering the trail system in a forested ridge linking to the greenbelt and Freiburg's surrounding countryside (Freiburg, 2008; Freiburg, 2011).

Vitoria-Gasteiz, Spain created its greenbelt by restoring former gravel pits, garbage dumps, a polluted river and a degraded wetland into five major parks that largely encircle the urban center. A network of bike paths extends through this greenbelt, providing planet-friendly transportation options as well as 91 kilometers for exercising close to nature. Vitoria's local planning think tank, the Environmental Studies Centre, refers to the greenbelt as an "eco-recreational corridor" within a green structure consisting of several concentric circles. Outside the greenbelt lies an agricultural belt covering 58 percent of the city's total land area. Beyond the agricultural belt is a green ring of forested mountains which have retained almost all of their native species due to protection from public ownership and ancient rules governing the use of water, pasturage and other resources. In turn, the forest ring links with natural spaces known as the Highland Belt and the pan-European ecological corridor that runs from the Galician mountains to the Alps (Environmental Studies Center, 2012; European Union, 2012; O'Neill & Rudden, 2010; Vitoria-Gasteiz, 2010; Vitoria Gasteiz, 2016).

In 1927, Essen, Germany adopted a green area system plan depicting inner and outer greenbelts connected by roughly 17 green corridors plus a dozen green fingers extending toward the city center. The southern greenbelt along the Ruhr River survived the 20th century largely as shown in the 1927 plan. Essen began implementing some of the plan's other components under a 1975 program that has created over 100 green areas on lands degraded and abandoned by coal mines and steelworks. Today, green areas and open space account for over half of the City's land area and Essen has recommitted to the goal of connecting its greenspace using a strategy called "Essen – New Ways to the Water", which places a 150-kilometer "Green main route network" within 500 meters of more than 250,000 residents. Three north-south corridors within this network link southern green areas along the Ruhr River with restoration projects north of the City including the Zollverine Coal Mine UNESCO World Heritage Site and Emscher Landscape Park, a regional project currently restoring what was once one of the most polluted rivers in Europe. As of 2014, over 500 projects had been implemented under New Ways to the Water (Essen, 2014; EGC, 2015).

Access by Proximity

Compact, multiple-use development reduces transportation problems simply by putting everything people need closer together, if not in the same place. Higher-density, diverse cities, when properly designed, make it easier for residents to get to work, schools, shopping and even greenspace without the need to use or perhaps even own a car. Richard Register, a pioneer in the ecocity movement and founder of Ecocity Builders, used the term "access by proximity" in his groundbreaking 1987 book *Ecocity Berkeley*: "Instead of thinking in terms of *going* places, think in terms of *being* places" (Register, 1987, p. 33). To this day, Register continues to emphasize this often-forgotten point: "It's said 'the fastest route from point A to point B is a straight line.' Not so. It is moving the points closer together" (Register, 2016).

All of the cities profiled in this book stress the significance of multiple-use density in their plans. In 1998, Munich, Germany adopted a new general plan built on three words: compact – urban - green. Recognizing that access by proximity is essential to all things sustainable, three cities in Germany, Heidelberg, Essen and Munster, all refer to themselves as "cities of short distances." The goal of compact cities is perhaps best illustrated in the following examples from Stockholm, Vitoria-Gasteiz, Bristol, Freiburg and Oslo.

In Stockholm, Sweden, the 1999 City Plan proclaimed that the urban form of this city was largely complete and declared that future growth would be accommodated by infill and brownfield redevelopment. This anti-sprawl goal has been memorialized in the phrase "build the city inwards." The city has achieved international recognition by transforming a formerly-polluted industrial area into a sustainability showcase. This eco-district, called Hammarby Sjostad, is so successful that it has become a tourist destination and an international calling card for Stockholm's green industries. As proof that the city is indeed growing inward, a 2013 study by the London School of Economics found that Stockholm surpassed the urban containment index of twelve comparably-sized cities (Floater, Rode and Zenghelis, 2013).

In Vitoria-Gasteiz, Spain, 81 percent of residents live within 1,500 meters of the city center even though population has tripled since the 1960s. The urban area represents less than 15 percent of the city's total land area but accommodates 98 percent of the population. Vitoria aims to retain its compact form by redeveloping underutilized properties at densities of up to 400 dwelling units per hectare and through a policy known as re-densification. These tactics are working. Between 2001 and 2010, 97 percent of growth occurred within the greenbelt (European Commission, 2010; European Union, 2012; Vitoria-Gasteiz, 2010).

In Bristol, United Kingdom, a 2007 policy channels all development away from greenfield locations and toward brownfield sites. Redevelopment projects here are largely succeeding in

Figure 1-4: The waterside walkways and public spaces of Harborside have revitalized downtown Bristol.

revitalizing a city center that was once highly-dependent on harbor-related industries that have mostly departed to larger ports. In the city center alone, 26 hectares of contaminated land were transformed into Harborside, a high-density, mixed use neighborhood with waterfront walkways, cycle paths and public spaces that are drawing people back to downtown living. As an indicator of success, 98 percent of business development and 94 percent of residential development occurred on brownfield sites between 2002 and 2012, a period in which population grew by ten percent (Bristol, 2012).

Freiburg, Germany curbs sprawl using "inner development", the redirection of growth to infill sites, particularly underutilized industrial areas and former military bases. In 2006, Freiburg adopted a land use plan that actually reduced the land designated for development. Using compact development, Freiburg estimates that up to 95 percent of growth to the year 2030 can be accommodated within the current city borders (Freiburg, 2008; Freiburg, 2011).

Oslo, Norway directs development to a waterfront district known as Fiord City where three eco-neighborhoods in various stages of revitalization are connected by a pedestrian/bicycle path called the Harbor Promenade. Oslo has the highest growth rate of all European capitals. Nevertheless, it succeeded in locating 80 percent of all growth occurring between 2002 and 2006 on brownfields and other previously-developed land (Oslo, 2009).

Feet First

When cities build compact, multiple-use centers, people have less need for cars and other forms of transportation because they can walk to jobs, shopping, schools and many other everyday destinations. In his inspirational yet practical book, *Walkable City*, Jeff Speck summarizes the importance of walkability this way:

> Walkability is both an end and a means, as well as a measure. While the physical and social rewards of walking are many, walkability is perhaps most useful as it contributes to urban vitality and most meaningful as an indicator of that vitality. After several decades spend redesigning pieces of cities, trying to make them more livable and more successful, I have watched my focus narrow to this topic as the one issue that seems to both influence and embody most of the others. Get walkability right and so much of the rest will follow (Speck, 2012,

page 4).

Walkability is easy to visualize but can be hard to accomplish. It requires the political will to prioritize people within the public right of way, ideally by completely pedestrianizing streets and sometimes entire neighborhoods. To repopulate streets with pedestrians, cities are also paying more attention to the quality of the streetscape in terms of scale, architectural diversity and landscape/hardscape design. Interesting examples of pedestrian friendliness can be found in Vitoria-Gasteiz, Barcelona, Copenhagen, Ljubljana, Freiburg, Salzburg, Heidelberg and Munich.

In Vitoria-Gasteiz, Spain, pedestrians get top priority. As mentioned above, a sprawl-curbing greenbelt and higher-density mixed use development have succeeded in putting 81 percent of the city's 242,000 people within 1,500 meters of the city center. In addition, the foundation of Vitoria's transportation strategy is super-blocks. These are actually mini-neighborhoods where the interior streets, called pedestrian-priority streets, are restricted to walkers, bicyclists, deliveries and motorists who live within the super-block. The maximum speed limit on a pedestrian-priority street is 10 kilometers per hour. This reconfiguration of the right of way converts 70 percent of the space previously reserved for cars into car-free public space. All other traffic is limited to the perimeter of the super-block on roadways called private vehicle primary streets. Eventually, Vitoria plans for over half of the roadway system to be pedestrian-priority streets. By combining compact development with pedestrian-friendly infrastructure, Vitoria has already built a city in which over half of all trips occur on foot (European Commission, 2010; European Union, 2012; Vitoria-Gasteiz, 2010).

People love to walk, particularly when the path is interesting as well as safe and when the walkway connects attractive destinations. Barcelona's mile-long La Rambla is a classic example. This pedestrian street links Catalonia Square, a major transportation hub, with the city waterfront using a tree-shaded promenade lined with outdoor cafes, book vendors and craft stalls. Motor vehicles travel on single one-way lanes flanking La Rambla but do not cross the pedestrian space. Prior to hosting the 1992 Olympics, Barcelona joined La

Rambla to La Rambla del Mar, a pedestrian bridge spanning part of the harbor and connecting with a former dock now retrofitted with public squares, entertainment venues and the city aquarium. From there, people can stroll around the marina and meander two more miles of restaurant-dotted boardwalk built on beachfronts that Barcelona created from a previously-derelict port district. The price tag for this pedestrian infrastructure and other improvements was hefty. But Barcelona is now the 5th most popular tourist destination in Europe (Iwamiya and Yeh, 2011; Taylor, 2012).

Figure 1-5: *La Rambla multitasks as a transportation, culture, entertainment and tourism magnet.*

Copenhagen, Denmark was a pioneer in the pedestrian streets movement. In 1962, the city banished non-essential motor vehicles from a one-kilometer segment of Stroget Street. Skeptics predicted disaster. But the car-free atmosphere attracted more walkers, creating what is now a thriving retail/entertainment district. In addition to restricting motorized traffic, Copenhagen pays close attention to the quality of streetscapes. Beginning with its first "public space – public life" study in 1968, Copenhagen has documented the benefits of designing streets with human scale, engaging facades, soft edges and other features that are now part of the official planning tool box. These techniques have been successfully transplanted to New York City, Melbourne and other cities around the world (Gehl, 2010).

Ljubljana, Slovenia designated its city center as an ecological zone in 2007, closing streets to motor vehicles with the exception of early-morning deliveries. By 2013, the City had expanded the pedestrian district to more than 30 streets, a 550-percent increase. These prohibitions created a quieter and more peaceful downtown, causing measurable decreases in noise levels as well as the more obvious benefits of greater safety, improved air quality and reduction of greenhouse gas emissions (O'Neill and MacHugh, 2013).

In 1973, Freiburg limited access on many streets in its city center to deliveries and the few cars owned by downtown residents. As a result, this historic district serves workers, shoppers, occupants and tourists alike, crowded with people rather than automobiles. At the other end of a tram ride lies Vauban, Germany's largest car-free development, where internal parking is prohibited and only eight percent of residents own cars. As further evidence of pedestrian prioritization, over 90 percent of Freiburg's citizens live in neighborhoods where vehicular speed in limited to 30 kilometers per hour, or less than 19 miles per hour (Berrini and Bono, 2010; Freiburg, 2011; Medearis and Daseking, 2012).

In the center of Salzburg, Austria, people still get around on foot, much as they did in Mozart's day. The Gothic buildings and other architectural gems of the Altstadt form the heart of a 236-hectare UNESCO World Heritage Site here that incorporates the Mirabell Gardens, the Salzach River and surrounding mountains. UNESCO's recognition is based in part on the integrity of the urban fabric, which is logically enhanced by the fact that Salzburg prohibits non-essential motor vehicles on more than five miles of pavement throughout the World Heritage Site (UNESCO, 2015a; UNESCO, 2015b).

In Heidelberg, Germany, the land use plan calls for continued conversion of streets from single-purpose motorways to "living space". As proof that walkability is desirable as well as possible, most streets in Heidelberg's Old Town are already car-less. Perhaps the best example is Hauptstrasse, a mile-long, pedestrianized "main street" that rivals Barcelona's La Rambla for diversity of uses, architectural interest and human scale. Other examples outside the historic district include the Kirchheim neighborhood where traffic calming measures create a pedestrian network between popular destinations on streets with maximum speeds of seven kilometers per hour or just over four miles per hour (Beatley, 2000; Heidelberg, 2007; James and Fereday, 1999).

In Munich's historic center, pedestrian streets surround Marienplatz, the public square in front of Munich's neo-Gothic town hall, and extend north to the massive Englisher Garden, which also offers its own 78-kilometer network of foot paths and cycle tracks. Just east of downtown Munich, pedestrians can stroll on over 40 miles of paths and bike-friendly roads along the Isar River that lead to the farms and woods in the surrounding greenbelt.

Eco-mobility

After World War II, most US cities began splitting neighborhoods with freeways and surrendering precious downtown space to parking. But in an ill-conceived attempt to accommodate cars, US cities only encourage more to come. In contrast, the communities profiled in this book recognize that cars are insatiable. In addition to the pedestrian features noted above, these cities invest in public transportation and bicycle infrastructure. They often impose speed limits that not only make walking and cycling safer but also motivate more people to kick their auto-dependency. Perhaps the best examples of building cities for people rather than cars can be found in Copenhagen, Stockholm, Vitoria-Gasteiz, Bristol, Nijmegen, Munster, Barcelona, Nantes, Freiburg, Heidelberg and Munich.

In the 1960s, Copenhagen flirted with car culture and even removed a few bike lanes. But realizing the absurdity of designing cities for cars, this city of 562,000 people changed course in the 1970s and 1980s. It converted car lanes and parking spaces to cycle tracks which now flank every major roadway. Maximum speed limits of 30 kilometers per hour (19 mph) or, in some cases, 15 kilometers per hour (9 mph), are enforced on all other streets and bikes are welcome on public transportation. This infrastructure, with a combined length of 411 kilometers, makes it easy for Copenhageners to safely, quickly and healthily commute "door-to-door" by bike. The city provides additional motivation by timing traffic signals to bicycle speeds, giving bikes a head start at traffic lights and removing snow from cycle tracks before car lanes. As a result, 62 percent of Copenhageners bike to work and Copenhagen is widely acknowledged as the most bike-friendly city in the world (Copenhagen, 2007; Copenhagen, 2011; Copenhagen, 2013; Copenhagen, 2015; Gehl, 2010; UCI, 2014).

At 760 kilometers, Stockholm has an even longer bike-lane network than Copenhagen. This city of 910,000 people also enforces a 30 kilometer-per-hour speed limit on local streets, which helps explain why Stockholm doubled its bike use between 1990 and 2008. In addition, Stockholm puts public transportation within 300 meters of 90 percent of city residents and covers cab fare if buses or trains are delayed more than 20 minutes. In 2007, Stockholm began imposing a congestion charge on vehicles entering and exiting the downtown, a move that decreased city center traffic by 20 percent and increased public transportation ridership by seven percent. Stockholm estimates that the congestion charge alone has annually reduced CO2 emissions by 10 to 15 percent, resulting in 30,000 fewer tons of CO2 emissions per year (Berrini and Bono, 2010; European Commission, 2010a; Floater, Rode and Zenghelis, 2013; Richelsen and Sohuus, 2010; Stockholm, 2008).

Vitoria-Gasteiz, Spain, achieved a 45 percent increase in public transportation ridership by building tram lines, improving bus service and adopting new parking regulations. In addition, Vitoria offers 97 kilometers of cycle lanes/paths in the urban area plus 91 kilometers of pedestrian/cycle paths in the greenbelt. Due to the compact form of this city of 242,000 people, bicyclists can use this cycling infrastructure to reach any destination within the urban area in 15 minutes or less (European Union, 2012; Vitoria-Gasteiz, 2010).

Between 2009 and 2011, Bristol, United Kingdom invested more than 20 million pounds in bicycling improvements, creating a system with 299 kilometers of cycle lanes. This city of 441,000 people is also in the process of imposing a speed limit of 20 miles per hour in all residential neighborhoods. These moves are credited with increasing cycling by 80 percent between 2004 and 2012. In 1982, Bristol and its partners used an abandoned rail corridor to build the Bristol and Bath Railway Path, now the most popular bike trail in the country.

Today, bikes on this rail trail carry more people than the trains that used to travel this right of way (Bristol, 2012; Sustrans, 2016).

Figure 1-6: *The Bristol and Bath Railway Path now transports more people than the trains that used to travel this right of way.*

In the Netherlands city of Nijmegen, bike lanes are physically separated from "access" streets and all other roadways, known as "traffic limited" streets, are subject to speed limits of 30 kilometers per hour (19 mph). This city of 171,000 people also provides parking for 5,200 bikes in the downtown and 8,700 bikes at the railroad station as well as 43 kilometers of bicycle superhighways. These are high-speed cycle paths that prioritize cyclists headed for nearby cities as well as universities and other major destinations within town. The people of Nijmegan have responded to the city's investment. Bicycles account for 64 percent of all commuter traffic here and represent 37 percent of all trips of 7.5 kilometers or less, a larger percent than cars (Bicycle Dutch, 2015; Bicycle Dutch, 2016a; Bicycle Dutch, 2016b; European Commission, 2016a; Nijmegen, 2015).

Munster, Germany also imposes a 30 kilometer per hour speed limit on all residential streets and offers a 450-kilometer bike path network in addition to 255 kilometers of cycle paths off of main roads. This city of 300,000 people built Germany's largest bike garage, which provides bicycle repair, sales and lockers as well as storage for 3,300 bicycles. This bike garage, the Radstation, is located next to Munster's train station and less than 1,000 feet from the Promenade, the 4.5-kilometer cycling-pedestrian path encircling the downtown on the site of the ancient town walls. The Promenade allows car-free access to bike routes that radiate from the city center in all directions. As in Nijmegen, more people commute by bicycle in Munster than by motor vehicles (Munster, 2009; Munster, 2016).

Barcelona, Spain, aggressively promotes bicycling as well as walking. Roughly 72 percent of residents live within 300 meters of Barcelona's bike network. In 2012, the Barcelona bike share system offered 6,000 bicycles at 420 stations and experienced 40,000 trips per day. Barcelona's eco-mobility investments continue to generate enviable mode split statistics showing 80 percent of all trips in this city are accomplished on foot, by bike or on public transportation (Barcelona, 2013; Barcelona Yellow, 2016).

In 1985, Nantes became the first French city to successfully launch modern tram service. By 2014, that tram line was carrying 120,000 passengers daily, making it the third busiest line in the country. Nantes now has three additional tram lines, commuter rail, water buses and a busway. As of 2009, 95 percent of Nantes' 285,000 people lived within 300 meters of high-frequency public transportation. In addition to 210 kilometers of waterside walks, Nantes built 470 kilometers of cycle paths or tracks and serves as a hub for long distance cycle routes including the 365-kilometer trail that follows the repurposed tow path of the Nantes-Brest Canal as well as the 3,653-kilometer EuroVelo Route connecting Nantes with Romania via nine separate countries (European Commission, 2010b; European Commission, 2016b; Nantes, 2010; Nantes, 2014).

Freiburg, Germany began reducing speed limits on non-arterial streets in the 1990s. Today, 90 percent of Freiburg's 220,000 residents live in neighborhoods with 30 kilometer per hour limits, a policy that has reduced noise while improving safety for pedestrians and bicyclists. Freiburg's 420-kilometer bike network incorporates 170 kilometers of bike paths, 120 kilometers of forest/service roads and 130 kilometers of bike-friendly streets. As a result, 30 percent of all Freiburg trips are done by bicycle and another 15 percent occur on foot (Freiburg, 2011; Medearis and Daseking, 2012).

In Heidelberg, Germany, traffic-calming strategies are credited with reducing accidents by 31 percent and casualties by 44 percent (Beatley, 2000). This city of 150,000 people limits traffic to seven kilometers per hour on some roads, a restriction that encourages pedestrian and bicycle use as well as reducing noise (James and Fereday, 1999). Likewise, Hamburg, Germany motivates cycling by enforcing a 30 kilometer per hour speed limit on almost half of its street system as well as offering 1,700 kilometers of cycle lanes and a bike share system logging more than two million trips per year (Hamburg, 2008; Union Cycliste Internationale, 2014). To reach its stated goal of becoming the cycling capital of Europe, Munich, Germany has established two bike sharing services and a 1,200-kilometer network of bicycle paths and lanes (Munich, 2010; Munich, 2016).

Biodiversity

The cities profiled in this book are largely growing up on previously-developed and often degraded land. Consequently, achieving biodiversity typically requires more than simply protecting existing natural areas. Many of these cities are restoring long-lost habitat by remediating brownfields and renaturing streams that prior generations channelized in a misguided attempt to control flood waters. As discussed above, most of these cities are implementing green structure plans that connect open space using greenways that provide wildlife corridors in addition to various other benefits like water management, ecomobility and car-free recreation for nature-loving humans. Noteworthy biodiversity efforts can be found in Essen, Vitoria-Gasteiz, Mollet del Valles, Nijmegen, Freiburg, Hamburg, Munich, Stockholm, Ljubljana, Salzburg and Heidelberg.

Essen, Germany has a long history with biodiversity. In addition to the comprehensive 1927 green area plan discussed above, Essen established its first nature reserve in 1939. In 2010, Essen signed the Biodiversity in Municipalities Declaration and today conservation protections apply to over 34 percent of the city, including 12 nature reserves and 49 protected landscapes. However, Essen also lies at the heart of the Ruhr Valley, at one time the largest concentration of coal and steel industries in the world. Since 1975, Essen has restored over 100 sites degraded by these industries and completed over 500 projects under its ambitious New Ways to the Water greenspace strategy. Perhaps the biggest challenge is the Emscher River, at one time used as a wastewater canal and considered the most polluted river in Germany. Together with five other municipalities, Essen is tackling Europe's most comprehensive river naturalization project, called Emscher Landscape Park. By 2020, this consortium will complete the restoration of what were once open sewers into near-natural meandering streams, helping to protect the 109 animal species and 1,500 plant species that live here, including 50 listed species. In addition to promoting biodiversity, Emscher Landscape Park will manage storm water naturally and create a trail system offering recreation, exercise and alternative transportation options for pedestrians and bicyclists (EGC, 2015; Essen, 2014; Treanor, Connolly and McEvoy, 2014).

In the process of assembling its greenbelt, Vitoria-Gasteiz, Spain also created nature preserves out of abused lands, polluted rivers and degraded wetlands. Along the northern segment of the greenbelt, Vitoria rebuilt the Zadorra River to manage storm water and improve stream quality as well as restore wildlife habitat, ultimately becoming a Natura 2000 site. Similarly, the city reengineered the hydrology and vegetation of the previously-disturbed Salburua Wetlands, now home to numerous endangered species including the European mink, one of the most threatened carnivores on the planet. Today, birds literally flock to Salburua, which has been listed as a Natura 2000 site and an internationally-significant Ramsar wetland. In addition, Vitoria's outermost greenbelt, the forests and mountains encircling the city, preserves 91 percent of its native species due to public ownership and traditions that respect the use of natural resources (Environmental Studies Center, 2012; European Union, 2012; O'Neill & Rudden, 2010; Vitoria-Gasteiz, 2010; Vitoria-Gasteiz, 2016).

Figure 1-7: Vitoria-Gasteiz restored Salburua, now a Ramsar wetland and home to numerous endangered species.

Mollet del Valles, Spain, ten miles north of Barcelona, preserves a 700-hectare area known as Gallecs that works as a park within an agricultural and ecological landscape. The city and its partners have rebuilt riverbanks and restored wetlands here in order to manage and treat storm water as well as create habitat for birds and other wildlife. A collaborative effort has also replanted previously degraded lands with indigenous vegetation. Emphasis on organic farming has generated a diverse ecosystem ranging from butterflies and other insects to reptiles, amphibians, bats, hedgehogs and over sixty bird species. Although most of Gallecs is actively farmed, forested or leased for individual garden plots, Mollet del Valles maintains a trail network where hikers and bicyclists can learn about responsible agriculture and ecology while enjoying healthy outdoor recreation. In a city of 52,000 people, the Gallecs open classroom attracts 700,000 visitors per year, suggesting that Mollet del Valles has developed a winning formula for engaging people in sustainability (Consorci de Gallecs, 2015; European Commission, 2015).

Bristol was an early adopter of wildlife protection in the United Kingdom and in 2008 adopted the Bristol Biodiversity Action Plan which has been recognized as a model by the national government. This plan aims to put people and nature closer together through the creation of 16 local nature reserves and the restoration of Bristol's waterways. The Bristol Wildlife Network now protects habitat and natural corridors on private as well as public land covering 27 percent of the city's total land area. The network includes portions of a bypass of the Avon River known as the Floating Harbor where restoration of former docklands and the introduction of buoyant reed beds have made the water safe for human swimmers as well as returning otter populations. Bristol and its partners are also safeguarding the rugged Avon Gorge, home to 27 species listed nationally as rare and threatened. Further upriver, Bristol protects portions of the Severn Estuary, which has been classified as a European Marine Site, Special Protection Area, Ramsar site and a Special Area of Conservation (Bristol, 2012).

Nijmegen, Netherlands, is currently completing a $465-million project to relocate old dikes, dig an additional channel and create an island in a segment of the Waal River that flows through the city. This project, known as Room for the River, primarily aims to protect Nijmegen from the increasingly high floodwaters resulting from climate change. However, Room for the River will also create parkland, civic space and more room for nature by restoring stream ecology and recreating 30 different types of habitat including mudflats, meadows and forests. Together with partners upstream and downstream, Nijmegen plans to repopulate the Waal River and its reengineered floodplain with species that once lived here, including sturgeon, beaver, sea eagles and otter. Room for the River has already won international awards for innovatively combining water management with urban redevelopment and environmental restoration (Climate Wire, 2012; HUD User, 2015; Nijmegen, 2015).

Freiburg, Germany owns almost one third of the land within its borders, including Germany's largest communal forest. Roughly 90 percent of the 5,139-hectare city forest is protected for nature conservation and almost half is designated as Natura 2000. On the southern edge of the city, Freiburg uses environment-friendly management to safeguard habitat for lynx, chamois, three-toed woodpeckers and over 120 endangered plant and animal species on Schauinsland Mountain, one of the highest peaks in the Black Forest. In 1997, Freiburg established a 44-square-kilometer landscape conservation area in a lowland forest called Mooswald, or moss woods. Today, Mooswald is part of the European Natura 2000 system, offering protection to rare species of beetles, bats and woodpeckers as well as an easy way for birders and others to get in touch with nature (Freiburg, 2011; Medearis and Daseking, 2012).

Hamburg's 31 nature reserves occupy roughly eight percent of the city's total land area, the highest percentage in Germany. The city's 36 landscape protection areas cover 19 percent of Hamburg, safeguarding ecological as well as cultural and other resources. Hamburg is currently restoring the health of the environmentally-significant Elbe Estuary while simultaneously growing the Port of Hamburg, which is Europe's third-busiest port and the source of over 150,000 jobs. The port and its partners have launched a unique contaminant remediation project and created the 137-square kilometer Hamburg Wadden Sea National Park in the Elbe Estuary, now a UNESCO world heritage site, which preserves the largest mudflat in the world and habitat for over 2,000 animal species (European Commission, 2009; European Commission, 2011; Hamburg, 2008; Hamburg, 2012; Hamburg Port Authority, 2013).

The tree-shaded paths flanking the Isar River create one of Munich's most prominent green corridors. However, the river itself has been dammed, channelized and dehydrated by engineering projects started in the 19th century. By the 1980s, many referred to the Isar as a "dead river". Today, dense development straightjackets much of the river in its current location. But Munich's 1995 Isar Plan aims to resurrect the river by improving its floodwater retention capacity, retooling the riverbanks for recreational greenspace, restoring swimmable water quality and reintroducing the natural floodplain dynamics needed for wildlife habitat. As of 2010, Munich had succeeded in vastly improving eight kilometers of the Isar, creating spawning beds for salmon and other fish as well as beaches, pools and islands that serve as a recreational refuge for the residents of the compact city center (Munich, 2010; Oppermann, 2005).

In many of the cities profiled in this book, biodiversity is a natural outgrowth of park and historic preservation efforts. Stockholm's 1000-plus parks and nature reserves occupy 40 percent of the City and shelter more than 1,500 species (European Commission, 2010.) More than 20 percent of Ljubljana is in some form of nature protection status, with Ljubljansko Barje landscape park alone protecting 135 square kilometers of wetlands, riparian forests and ecologically-cultivated farmlands (EGC, 2014; Ljubljana, 2013). A UNESCO World Heritage Site protects 236 hectares of Salzburg including Kuputzinerberg Mountain which offers habitat to deer, badgers, martens and chamois, a species of goat-antelope native to the European mountains (UNESCO, 2015). From Heidelberg's old town, hikers can climb the Philosopher's Walk into UNESCO's Geo-Naturepark Bergstrasse-Odenwald, which conserves the biodiversity of 3,500 square kilometers of countryside bounded by the Rhine, Main and Neckar rivers (EGN, 2013; EGN, 2016).

Brownfields to Ecodistricts

The cities profiled in this book convert abandoned or underutilized industrial areas, harbors, rail yards and military bases into models of sustainability. These eco-neighborhoods or ecodistricts often showcase cutting edge planning, architecture and technology while achieving other goals for compactness, ecomobility, climate action and green structure. As sustainability incubators, these cities are attracting green innovators and entrepreneurs that greatly benefit local and regional economies. Some of the best examples can be found in Freiburg, Stockholm, Hamburg, Nantes, Oslo, Heidelberg, Helsinki, Copenhagen, Bristol, Essen, Munich, Salzburg, Munich and Nijmegen.

Freiburg turned a former military base into the Vauban neighborhood, Germany's largest car-free development. Only eight percent of residents here own cars, which they have to park in structures at the perimeter of the complex. Consequently, most residents prefer to commute using public transportation including a tram line directly linking the interior of Vauban with downtown Freiburg. Many dwelling units here use passive solar and a carbon-neutral cogeneration plant supplies heating as well as electrical power to 700 households. Ubiquitous rooftop photovoltaic solar collectors also create enough electricity to power 200 dwelling units. Perhaps most importantly, Vauban is a pleasant place to live, with gardens, landscaped courtyards and people-centric streets where residents can safely walk or bike to schools, shopping, entertainment venues, community centers and nearby tram stops (Berrini and Bono, 2010; Freiburg, 2011; Medearis and Daseking, 2012).

Stockholm, Sweden transformed a highly-contaminated industrial waterfront into Hammarby Sjostad, a model ecodistrict that tests innovative eco-technology without sacrificing the comfortable feel of a traditional neighborhood. The overriding goal is to cut environmental impacts in half using closed-loop energy, waste and water systems. The 11,000 apartments here are served by a district heating-cooling and electrical generation system that partly uses energy extracted from treated wastewater and solid waste combustion. The advanced wastewater treatment system creates a biogas that powers many Hammarby stoves and ranges as well as buses. Hammarby also makes extensive use of solar panels to heat water and generate electricity. The storm water management system is referred to as "architectonic" because of its aesthetic as well as practical benefits. Storm water is partially retained by green roofs and the residual is channeled into small canals lined with plants that create a landscaping feature while also treating contaminants. Fingers of greenspace reach into every part of Hammarby and link to a nearby nature reserve using a landscaped viaduct called an "ecoduct". Light rail, bus and ferry lines as well as pedestrian trails and cycle tracks make it possible for Hammarby residents to live car-free. In fact, 80 percent of Hammarby residents walk, bike or use public transportation (Floater, Rode and Zenghelis, 2013; Franne, 2007; OECD, 2013; Richelsen and Sohuus, 2010; Stockholm, 2015; URBED/TEN Group, 2011).

Hamburg is containing sprawl by converting obsolete industrial, port, rail, post office and military facilities into sustainable neighborhoods. HafenCity, a former dock and industrial area, is now a 155-hectare ecodistrict planned for 12,000 residents and 45,000 jobs located minutes away from downtown Hamburg via metro rail and served by a district heating system fueled by renewable energy sources. Described as a "City of Plazas, Parks and Promenades", 37 percent of HafenCity is publicly-owned or publically-accessible open space. HafenCity is also the home of Hamburg's newest architectural icon, Elbe Philharmonic Hall, which perches atop an old warehouse and ranks as Hamburg's tallest occupied building (European Commission, 2011; Hamburg, 2008; Kreutz, 2010).

Ecodistrict Ile de Nantes, one of three eco-neighborhoods in Nantes, France, revitalizes an island in the Lorie River that once housed a foundry, ship building yard and other port-related industries. Mixing worksites, retail and civic space as well as residences, this project uses a district heating network fueled by waste and wood, solar thermal installations, photovoltaics and an aerothermal heat pump. Some of the former industrial structures here have been repurposed as landscape architecture, including the Foundries Garden, which houses 200 trees and 100 plant varieties within the girders and furnaces once used to forge propellers. The former shipyards are now the home of Island Machines, a truly unique enterprise that builds whimsical animated artworks including a mechanical elephant that lumbers around the island carrying more than a dozen passengers on its back (Hure, 2013; Nantes, 2010).

Figure 1-8: *Oslo transformed a former shipyard into the walkable, high-density mixed use neighborhood of Aker Brygge.*

Since the 1980s. Oslo, Norway has been concentrating growth in Fiord City, a string of waterfront sites no longer needed for port-related industries. The first phase, Aker Brygge, turned a former shipyard into a high-density district of residences, offices, restaurants and public spaces designed for maximum walkability. Across a pedestrian bridge, the next phase, Tjuvholmen, features similarly compact mixed-use development anchored by a luxury hotel and an art museum designed by Renzo Piano. Oslo is currently completing phase three, Bjorvika, which positions high rise residential and office towers next to the central train station. On the fiord itself, the city's opera house invites people to climb around the marble-clad roof to get a 360-degree view of Oslo's spectacular setting between the blue of the water and the green of the forests (Gehl, 2010; Oslo, 2009).

Heidelberg's Bahnstadt converts a former railroad freight yard into an ecodistrict that blends residential units with office space, schools, movie theaters, kindergartens, retail stores and a private university. The futuristic Sky Labs building here welcomes science and technology innovators. Compact, mixed-use design emphasizes eco-mobility and Bahnstadt further pushes the energy-conservation envelope by requiring all buildings to meet extremely low "passive house" efficiency standards. With an area of 116 hectares, Bahnstadt becomes the world's largest passive house district (Heidelberg, 2007; Lisella, 2014; Passive House Institute, 2014).

In Helsinki, Finland, the relocation of port facilities from the city center creates infill sites for sustainable developments close to downtown. A former harbor/warehouse/industrial district became Ruoholahti, now home to 6,000 residents and 12,000 jobs served by buses, trams and metro rail. To enhance Ruoholahti's waterfront image, the city built a canal flanked by greenspace and pedestrian paths that link playgrounds and other amenities here. On the other side of downtown, Helsinki converted a former ceramics manufacturing complex and its environs into the Arabianranta district with the goal of creating the Baltic region's preeminent center for art and design. As of 2009, Arabianranta was home to three art libraries, the largest art university in the Nordic countries, an art museum/gallery, a conservatory and a public art trail funded by a percent-for-art requirement. Arabianranta also showcases earth-friendly design including waterfront raingardens that capture and treat runoff before it reaches the Vantaa River and the nearby Lammasarri Natura 2000 site (Helsinki, 2009; Jaakkola, 2012; Jokinen, 2015).

Copenhagen concentrates earth-friendly growth as close as

possible to the city center on remediated industrial, military, port, and rail facilities. From the Orestad neighborhood, a portion of which was previously military property, residents reliably reach downtown in less than ten minutes on high-frequency metro trains. To reduce commuting time even more, Orestad is steadily growing its own job sites including the headquarters of the Danish broadcasting corporation and Copenhagen Concert Hall. Orestad incorporates generous amounts of landscaped open space as well as protected wetlands and a storm water management system called SUDS. The Sustainable Urban Drainage System, or SUDS, locally treats runoff from roadways before adding it to rooftop discharge and releasing both to the meandering canals that add recreational options for residents and complement Orestad's overall design (Copenhagen, 2011; Copenhagen, 2012; European Commission, 2012).

As detailed in later chapters, all of the other cities in this book have their own brownfield redevelopment stories to tell. Bristol transformed 26 hectares of contaminated land into Harborside, a high density, mixed use project with waterside walkways, cycle paths and lively public spaces including the city's new central plaza, Millennium Square (Bristol, 2012). Essen converted a former railroad freight yard immediately north of downtown into Green Centre of Essen – University District, which combines residential, commercial and office uses close to cultural venues, shopping, the city's central public transportation hub and the Rhine Rail cycle trail (Essen, 2014). Munich retooled its old airport into Messestadt Riem, a new town with subway service and an extensive bike/pedestrian trail network that protects half of its 560-hectare area in open space while using the other half to accommodate an expected 14,000 people and 20,000 jobs (Munich, 2004). Salzburg changed an area that included its former soccer stadium into a mixed use district showcasing the energy savings achievable by retrofitting existing structures, erecting highly-efficient new buildings and employing alternative technologies including a thermal solar energy plant connected to a local district heating system (Bahr, 2014). Munster redeveloped former military grounds into Car-Free Garden City Weissenburg where residents cannot own cars yet can easily get to work and shopping using public transportation, Munster's extensive bicycle network and a car sharing station located at the edge of the project (Baumer, 2009; Munster 2016). In Nijmegen, the Hessenberg project turned a former newspaper/printing complex into a ten-building mini-neighborhood of apartments and retail space within an intricate network of gardens, courtyards and pedestrian alleyways reflecting this district's pre-automobile configuration (Europaconcorsi. 2015; Nijmegen, 2015).

Climate Action and Alternative Energy

Ecocities use a wide range of strategies to minimize the greenhouse gas emissions that cause climate change. They weatherize existing buildings and erect new structures that employ advanced solar, photovoltaic and district heating/cooling technologies. The cities profiled in this book also generate heat and power using wind, water, geothermal, biogas, biomass and other planet-friendly fuels. Many have pledged to meet ambitious deadlines for becoming carbon neutral and are making huge investments to meet those targets. Some of the most aggressive programs are located in Stockholm, Hamburg, Copenhagen, Freiburg, Nijmegen, Bristol, Essen, Heidelberg, Oslo, Torres Vedras, Munster and Ljubljana.

Between 1990 and 2005, Stockholm cut per capita greenhouse gas emissions by 25 percent largely through the use of renewable energy in its district heating network, which served 80 percent of the city in 2015. District cooling systems alone reduce CO_2 emissions by 60,000 tons per year here. Stockholm is also testing closed-loop technologies in its ecodistricts including Hammarby Sjostad, where energy from wastewater and solid waste combustion generates electricity and powers a district heating and cooling district system serving 11,000 households. In addition, Stockholm reduces emissions using compact development served by extensive public transportation and bikeway networks. Based on its progress to date, Stockholm aims to be fossil fuel free by 2040 (Berrini and Bono, 2010; European Commission, 2010; Floater, Rode and Zenghelis, 2013; Frane, 2007; Stockholm, 2008; Stockholm, 2015).

Hamburg reduced per-capita CO_2 emissions over 25 percent between 1990 and 2005 by launching renewable energy projects, forming energy-saving partnerships with private industry and expanding its already-green transportation infrastructure, which locates high-frequency public transit within 300 meters of almost all Hamburg households. Leading by example, the city cut energy use in

65,000 units of public housing, fuels power generators and district heating networks with municipal waste and sponsors attention-getting projects like Energy Bunker which converted a World War II flak tower into an alternative energy showcase featuring photovoltaics and a massive reservoir heated by solar thermal, biomass, wood and waste heat from a nearby industrial plant. In 2003, the City and its partners launched the Eco-Partnership Project, a public-private effort that uses various incentives to annually save 163,700 tons of carbon emissions, 26,500 tons of waste and 712,300 cubic meters of water (Berrini and Bono, 2010; Dezeen, 2014; European Commission, 2011; Hamburg, 2008; Hamburg, 2012; Hamburg, 2015; Hamburg, 2016).

Copenhagen aims to be the world's first carbon free capital by 2025. In less than ten years, Copenhagen plans to be a net exporter of power from a biomass and wind-based system. To meet that goal, the city committed to installing 30,000 square meters of photovoltaic panels on municipal buildings and erecting 100 wind turbines with a combined capacity of 360 MW. Experts believe that Copenhagen will hit its 2025 target given the fact that the City cut carbon emissions a remarkable 40 percent between 1995 and 2012. Much of this reduction resulted from switching from coal to biomass in the combined heating and power districts that serve 98 percent of all households in the City. In addition, Copenhagen seems to thrive on its carbon diet: between 2005 and 2014, City population rose by 15 percent and its economy grew by 18 percent while its carbon emissions fell by 31 percent (Copenhagen, 2011; Copenhagen, 2015; European Commission, 2012; European Commission, 2014; O'Neill and Rudden, 2012).

For decades, Freiburg has been at the forefront of energy conservation and alternative energy technologies. This city of 220,000 people created Germany's first passive solar high rise building as part of the energy retrofit of an entire 2,000-household neighborhood. As of 2009, over 1,000 photovoltaic collectors covered the rooftops of Freiburg's public and private buildings. Perhaps the most famous symbols of "Solar City" Freiburg are the photovoltaic array atop the soccer stadium and Heliotrope, the completely solar-powered 1994 house that rotates for maximum sunlight capture. Not content with these accomplishments, Freiburg aims to put solar collectors on every home in the City. In fact, if solar panels are not installed on a new dwelling, the city requires that the roof at least be built to accommodate solar photovoltaic or thermal systems in the future. As of 2009, Freiburg's 140 cogeneration plants produced roughly half of the city's power and district heating needs. The city relies heavily on hydropower as well as solar and biomass, powering its extensive tram network entirely by renewable energy. In a possibly unique application, seven small hydroelectric plants are partly fed by the "Bachle", the tiny water canals that Freiburg restored within the streets of the pedestrian zone of the historic city center (Freiburg, 2011).

Between 2008 and 2014, Nijmegen reduced per capita carbon emissions over 16 percent partly by gaining energy-conservation commitments from the city's largest companies and institutions including public utilities and the city itself. These commitments alone saved almost 300,000 tons of CO2. Currently, Nijmegen is converting a huge coal fired power plant on the Waal River to an alternative energy showcase featuring solar, wind, biomass and other renewable energy sources. In the longer term, Nijmegen is implementing an ambitious plan to install 16 wind turbines, a million solar panels and 40,000 solar boilers as well as a district heating network for 11,000 households plus increased reliance on biomass and geothermal, all with the goal of being energy-neutral by 2045 (European Commission, 2016; Nijmegen, 2015).

In 2000, Bristol became the United Kingdom pilot for ICLEI's Cities for Climate Protection program. By 2009, the City surpassed the targets established by the European Union and United Kingdom, aiming for a 40 percent carbon-emission reduction by 2020 and an 80 percent reduction by 2050 using a 2005 baseline. Between 2005 and 2010, Bristol lowered its emissions 19 percent, achieving the lowest CO2 emissions per capita of all major cities in the country. Leading by example, Bristol installed the first city-owned wind farm in the United Kingdom and also became the first city in the country to fuel its boilers with wood waste from its own parks and street trees. All new developments here are required to install on-site renewable-energy sources capable of achieving emission-reduction goals that are 20 percent more ambitious than the national code. A complex here called CO2 Zero was the first residential development and the first live-work development in the country to achieve a near-zero standard for heating, light and ventilation (Bristol, 2012; United Kingdom,

2009).

Figure 1-9: Torres Vedras is on its way to generating all of its electricity by wind power.

Essen, Germany targets carbon emission reductions of 40 percent by 2020 and 95 percent by 2050 compared with 1990, which is substantially more ambitious than the goals established by the European Union, Germany and the State of North Rhine-Westphalia. To reach these targets, Essen formed an independent Climate Agency which helps building owners analyze, plan, finance and complete energy retrofits. Leading by example, the city itself uses 100 percent green electricity in its operations and requires all of its new buildings to meet passive house standards. The 17 buildings in Essen's Gruga Park are served by a local heating district fueled entirely by the park's garden wastes. Essen also uses domestic waste in a waste-to-energy plant that generates electricity as well as enough heat to meet 20 percent of the City's total demand through the city's district heating system (EGC, 2015; Essen, 2014; O'Toole, McEvoy and Campion, 2015).

In 2000, Heidelberg, Germany formed an Energy Efficiency Agency tasked with saving 6 million kWh annually by retrofitting three percent of the region's older buildings every year. In addition to cutting carbon emissions, this program was projected to create 1,100 jobs and inject 110 million euros of direct investment into the local economy. Heidelberg also uses alternative energy in city-owned properties, with the extra revenue to the city's power supplier reinvested in renewable-energy improvements including photovoltaic systems on schools and a biogas heat/power plant at the zoo fueled by animal waste (Herrmann, 2002; ICLEI, 2007).

All of the other cities profiled in this book also pursue strategies to curb greenhouse gas emissions. Oslo generates almost all of its power hydroelectrically and it aims to further cut fossil fuel use by expanding its district heating system using waste-to-energy and bioenergy plants (European Commission, 2009; Oslo 2008). Torres Vedras, Portugal already harnesses coastal breezes in nine wind farms and plans to expand turbine capacity to 332 GWh, which would supply the city's entire electrical energy demand (Torres Vedras, 2014). In 2015, Munster became the first German city to divest its pension fund of oil, gas and all other fossil fuels, explaining that such investments are incompatible with the City's climate protection goals (Mattauch, 2015). Ljubljana, Slovenia targets up to an 80-percent reduction in greenhouse gas emissions between 2008 and 2050 by using a combination of compact growth, energy conservation and a transportation strategy in which public transport and non-motorized travel account for twice as many trips as cars by the year 2020 (EGC, 2014).

Public Engagement

Sustainability cannot be achieved by relying solely on improvements in public transportation, bike networks, alternative energy generation and other eco-infrastructure. Personal behavior is just as important (Moore, 2015). For a new tram line to reduce carbon emissions, for example, people have to ride it. Consequently, the European Green Capitals program asks applicants how they are engaging citizens in planning their communities and motivating them to lead planet-friendly lives. Some cities that are nurturing greener lifestyles include Helsinki, Essen, Nantes, Torres Vedras, Freiburg, Mollet del Valles and Salzburg.

Helsinki's Eco-Viikki, Finland's largest sustainability laboratory, incorporates homes, schools and day care centers within an easy walk or bike ride from shopping, jobs and the science campus of the University of Finland. The buildings here, bristling with solar collectors and photovoltaic panels, are separated by linear open spaces that maximize solar access and passive recreation while managing rainwater retention for use in individual garden plots for nearby residents. However, even the greenest community will not succeed without the cooperation of its inhabitants. As noted by Eco-Viikki's Project Manager: "... sustainability of a residential area depends first of all on the lifestyle of its inhabitants" (Helsinki, 2010; Joss, 2011; Rinne, 2009).

Figure 1-10: *Helsinki's Eco-Viikki neighborhood engages residents in extremely local agriculture as well as recycling, alternative energy, water management and sustainable lifestyles.*

In naming the winner of the 2017 European Green Capital award, the European Commission praised Essen, Germany for accomplishments in climate action, noise abatement, waste reduction, brownfield revitalization and the growth of a greenway network connecting largely-restored open space areas constituting over half the land area of the City. Importantly, the European Commission noted that while the city has led by example, it has also focused on public education and citizen involvement in its sustainability planning and implementation: "The City is making admirable efforts to establish itself as a 'City in transformation' that is overcoming a challenging history to reinvent itself as a 'Green City' and a leading example for others. The City credits its citizens and their ability to change as key to this success and this ethos is visible through their application tag line "ESSENtials – changing the way we act"" (EGC, 2015).

Similarly, Nantes' winning application for the 2013 European Green Capital award stressed that "cities will not achieve their objectives without the citizens." In that year, the city sent its green message into the streets using a fanciful 53-foot high Flying Greenhouse powered by on-board composting. Nantes families compete in neighborhood teams to show how they can pursue international carbon reduction goals using practical, measurable and sociable activities. The Nantes Exhibition Center also hosts learning experiences like "my life – my town – my planet" that help students understand the connection between their actions and the health of Mother Earth (Nantes, 2010; European Commission, 2016).

Torres Vedras uses its Center for Environmental Education to showcase green technology and engage students in sustainable living programs (Torres Vedras, 2014). In Freiburg, 50 schools, churches and other groups have become stream sponsors, which often involves the removal of invasive species and the restoration of native aquatic habitat (Freiburg, 2011). In Mollet del Valles, an estimated 700,000 people per year visit Gallecs and many undoubtedly learn a thing or two about organic agriculture, sustainable forestry and biodiversity while enjoying the miles of trails in this outdoor classroom (Consorci de Gallecs, 2015). In Salzburg, residents were fully involved in planning the transformation of a district of neglected buildings into the revitalized Lehen district featuring energy-efficient residences served by neighborhood facilities including a public library and elderly daycare center (Bahr, 2014).

Green is Good

Critics sometimes argue that we cannot afford sustainability no matter how appealing and rational it may sound. Many of the cities in this book illustrate that we cannot afford to reject sustainability. Some of these cities are getting more prosperous because their pioneering work is growing exportable green sector goods, technology and expertise that increase job opportunities and expand the local economy. In addition, the greenspace, bike culture and diverse centers of ecocities are likely to attract innovators, entrepreneurs, investors and other members of the creative class essential to a post-industrial economy. Freiburg, Copenhagen, Hamburg, Stockholm, Bristol, Nantes, Ljubljana and Torres Vedras are among the cities proving that healthy economies are possible not just despite sustainability efforts but also because of these initiatives.

Freiburg's economy has benefited handsomely from the city's early commitment to sustainability in general and solar energy in particular. Europe's largest institute for applied solar energy research was launched here in 1981 and today it consults around the world with a staff of 800 employees. In addition, 2,000 solar enterprises now operate in the Freiburg region generating 650 million euros annually and employing 12,000 workers. Each year, an estimated 25,000 academics, students, researchers and other "specialist tourists" come to see Freiburg's success firsthand, increasing eco-tourism income. Green-leaning visitors are often so impressed that they move here, an in-migration that at least boosts support for the city's sustainability goals and in some cases leads to new businesses (Freiburg, 2011; Rohracher and Spath, 2012).

By pushing the green envelope, Copenhagen and Denmark as a whole have added new, growth industries to their economies. In 2010, the Danish wind industry employed 25,000 workers and was growing by 30 percent every year. The green sector as a whole in the Copenhagen Region grew 55 percent between 2005 and 2009 and is now seen as an important wealth generator and economic engine.

Public-private partnerships have formed to help firms profit from this momentum, including Green Businesses, a network of almost 1,000 companies working here on noise reduction, air pollution and water contamination as well as fossil fuel consumption (Copenhagen, 2011; Copenhagen, 2015).

Hamburg is expanding its already substantial industrial sector using incentives and regulations to maximize energy efficiency and minimize waste of all kinds. As of 2009, more than 600 renewable energy companies were located in and around Hamburg. The city grows its exportable expertise through the Hamburg Renewable Energy Cluster which facilitates networking between local firms, institutions, universities and NGOs to inspire and support enhanced research and development. By 2011, two global manufacturers of wind turbines located in Hamburg and the Renewable Energy Cluster had grown to 163 companies, putting Hamburg on the map as a world center for alternative energy innovation (European Commission, 2011; Hamburg, 2012).

Stockholm's Hammarby Sjostad ecodistrict develops and tests alternative technologies in search of new ways to cut environmental impacts in half using closed-loop energy, waste and water systems.

Figure 1-11: *The eco-innovations of Hammarby Sjostad create an international calling card for Stockholm's engineers, architects and planners.*

The success of Hammarby and Stockholm's other planet-friendly initiatives has nurtured a workforce with green expertise and skills in advance of growing worldwide demand for sustainable development. Hammarby alone attracts 10,000 visitors every year, an indication of how Stockholm has effectively branded itself as a pioneer in this field. A study by the London School of Economics found Stockholm to be one of the world's leading cities in the development of ecodistricts and green solutions, expertise that can be marketed internationally and used to attract investment, innovators and skilled professionals in a "…virtuous cycle of green growth" (Floater, Rode and Zenghelis, 2013; Franne, 2007).

Like Stockholm, other cities profiled in this book attract new residents and well as international visitors with their focus on sustainability. Due to its highly educated work force, Bristol has landed many leading environmental organizations like City Farms, Forum for the Future, the Schumacher Institute and the national headquarters of the Environment Agency (Sawday, 2012). In 2013 alone, Nantes hosted over 20 international events on sustainability issues including the World Mayor's Summit on Climate Change and the Ecocity World Summit (Nantes, 2014). The greening of Ljubljana helped this Slovenian city double tourist visits between 2002 and 2014 (Ljubljana Tourism, 2016). In addition to promoting its beaches and historic monuments, Torres Vedras uses an energy and tourism tech trail to attract visitors interested in learning about this city's progress in energy conservation and eco-mobility as well as wind power (Portugal, 2015).

CHAPTER 2

Stockholm, Sweden – Build the city inwards

Stockholm's won its position as a sustainability leader by starting early and never resting. The form of this city of 910,000 largely follows public transportation corridors, leaving large swaths of greenspace in between for the enjoyment of residents as well as wildlife. To retain this compact shape, Stockholm directs much of its strong growth pressure into brownfields and other redevelopment sites, experimenting with cutting edge environmental technologies and producing results, like Hammarby Sjostad, that serve as international models. Today, Stockholm is steadily decreasing its CO2 emissions using green transportation strategies, alternative energy and by continually expanding a district heating network that already serves 80 percent of the city. In recognition, Stockholm was named the first European Green Capital in 2010.

In the 1950s, Stockholm responded to a surge in growth demand by building 25 communities with populations of about 10,000 each around its new metro system (Lantz, 2001). Stockholm has largely retained this regional form by keeping development within public transportation corridors and retaining the spaces in between them. In the 1990s, the Stockholm Regional Planning Office stressed the significance of these green wedges for biodiversity, outdoor

Figure 2-1: *The architectonic storm water system, and overall attention to desgn, make Hammarby Sjostad attractive as well as sustainable*

recreation and other environmental benefits. Today, from 20 to 30 percent of these areas are protected in eight nature reserves. The remainder is under private or institutional ownership but designated as green wedges in the regional plan and in the plans of the region's 26 municipalities. The 2010 regional plan advocates additional long term protection, with the goal of making the city "never far from nature". On the theory that people will save what they love, planners also promote ways of improving public access to the green wedges on foot, by bike and using public transportation improvements called green hubs (Akerlund, 2011; Floater, Rode and Zenghelis, 2013; Lekberg, 2010; Nelson, undated; Office of Regional Planning, 2010).

Many of Stockholm's green wedges extend into the city center, including the Jarva Wedge, home to National City Park (Lekberg, 2010). Established in 1994, National City Park is said to be the world's first national urban park. It is home to hundreds of cultural and historic landmarks including four royal palaces. But it also goes by the name Ekoparken and provides habitat for old oaks and wildlife ranging from deer and rabbits to rare species. In total, Stockholm's 1000+ parks and nature reserves occupy 40 percent of the City and shelter more than 1,500 species. Roughly 90 percent of the population lives within 300 meters of a green area (European Commission, 2010.)

To protect greenspace and create a vibrant, sustainable city, Stockholm aims to "build the city inwards." The 1999 City Plan saw the Stockholm's urban form as essentially complete and called for concentration of future growth in the city center and revitalized brownfields. A 2013 study by the London School of Economics found that Stockholm has been quite successful in containing growth within its urban core, surpassing the urban containment index of twelve comparably-sized cities (Floater, Rode and Zenghelis, 2013). Between 2000 and 2007, 30 percent of the growth in Stockholm occurred on brownfields (Berrini and Bono, 2010).

Stockholm's most famous brownfield redevelopment is Hammarby Sjostad, on a lakeside site that was once occupied by small but highly-polluting industrial uses. The City proposed a model eco-village here in an attempt to win the 2004 Summer Olympic Games. Even though Stockholm lost that bid, they decided to build a state-of-the-art ecodistrict anyway designed to cut environmental impacts in half using closed-loop energy, waste and water systems

(Floater, Rode and Zenghelis, 2013; Richelsen and Sohuus, 2010; Stockholm, 2015; URBED/TEN Group, 2011).

Hammarby residents themselves generate half of their energy needs. The 11,000 apartments here are served by a district heating and cooling system that partly uses energy extracted from treated wastewater and solid waste combustion, which is also used to produce electricity. The advanced wastewater treatment system creates a biogas that powers many Hammarby stoves and ranges as well as buses. Hammarby uses solar panels to heat water and generate electricity. Light rail, bus and ferry lines as well as pedestrian trails and cycle tracks make it possible for Hammarby residents to live car-free. In fact, 80 percent of Hammarby residents walk, bike or use public transportation (Floater, Rode and Zenghelis, 2013; Franne, 2007).

Figure 2-2: *Light rail service to downtown helps Hammarby residents live car-free.*

Attention to open space and design keeps Hammarby from seeming like a technology exhibition. The storm water management system is referred to as "architectonic" because of its aesthetic as well as practical benefits. Storm water is partially retained by green roofs and the residual is channeled into small canals lined with plants that create a landscaping feature while also treating contaminants. Fingers of greenspace reach into every part of Hammarby and link to a nearby nature reserve using a landscaped viaduct called an "ecoduct". Experts, including the Office of Economic Cooperation and Development, recognize Hammarby as a model ecodistrict (OECD, 2013). It has also become an economic development tool, attracting 10,000 visitors every year and creating an international clientele for the architects, contractors and technicians who helped build it (Floater, Rode and Zenghelis, 2013; Franne, 2007).

Stockholm wants to top the accomplishments of Hammarby Sjostad with its Royal Seaport ecodistrict, which will transform 236 hectares of former harbor, oil and gas facilities into a mixed-use complex combining boat terminals, offices, retail, green space and 12,000 residences. Royal Seaport will serve as a laboratory for sustainability innovations involving closed-loop systems, climate change adaptations and alternative energy technologies, including district heating and electricity powered by biofuels. The Royal Seaport is one of 18 projects in the world to receive funding from Climate Positive, a joint program of the Clinton Climate Initiative and the US Green Building Council. Upon its scheduled completion in 2030, Stockholm Royal Seaport aims to be fossil fuel free (Floater, Rode and Zenghelis, 2013; Stockholm, 2016).

Stockholm gets high marks for cutting the greenhouse gas emissions that produce climate change. Between 1990 and 2005, Stockholm reduced its per-capita CO_2 emissions by 25 percent. Much of the credit goes to Stockholm's district heating network, which the City launched over half a century ago. In 2008, 70 percent of the City was served by district heating and 70 percent of district heat was generated by renewable fuels including biogas from wastewater treatment plants. District cooling systems also contribute an annual reduction of 60,000 tons of CO_2. Stockholm is continually expanding its district heating and cooling system. In fact, by 2015, Stockholm reported that 80 percent of all buildings were connected to district heating (Berrini and Bono, 2010; European Commission, 2010; Stockholm, 2008; Stockholm, 2015).

Stockholm also put its transportation system on a CO_2 diet. Roughly 90 percent of Stockholm residents live within 300 meters of

Figure 2-3: *National City Park, part of the 40 percent of Stockholm in greenspace.*

public transportation. To instill confidence, Stockholm pays for a taxi if your bus or train is delayed more than 20 minutes. As an added incentive to use public transportation, Stockholm imposes a congestion charge on vehicles entering or exiting the inner city zone on weekdays. Since instituting the congestion charge in 2007, city center traffic has dropped 20 percent and public transportation ridership has increased by seven percent. Stockholm estimates that the congestion charge alone has annually reduced CO_2 emissions by 10 to 15 percent, resulting in 30,000 fewer tons of CO_2 emission per year (Floater, Rode and Zenghelis, 2013; Richelsen and Sohuus, 2010; Stockholm, 2008).

Despite its harsh winters, Stockholm doubled bicycle use between 1990 and 2008. Stockholm motivates cycling by offering more than 760 kilometers of bike lanes, which on a per-capita basis is higher than Amsterdam and Copenhagen. Even when bike lanes are not available, Stockholm promotes cycling by enforcing a 30 kilometer per hour speed limit on local streets (Berrini and Bono, 2010; European Commission, 2010; Stockholm, 2008).

Stockholm proves that a city can grow its population and economy while simultaneously weaning itself from fossil fuels (OECD, 2013). Furthermore, a study by the London School of Economics found Stockholm to be one of the world's leading cities in the development of ecodistricts and green solutions, expertise that can be marketed internationally and used to attract investment, innovators and skilled professionals in a "...virtuous cycle of green growth" (Floater, Rode and Zenghelis, 2013 p38).

Most importantly, Stockholm's sustainability goals are becoming even more ambitious. When it was named Europe's first Green Capital in 2010, the City was aiming to be fossil fuel free by 2050 (Stockholm, 2008). When it submitted its five-year follow-up report in 2015, Stockholm had moved that deadline forward, committing to be fossil fuel free by 2040 (Stockholm, 2015).

CHAPTER 3

Hamburg, Germany: The business of sustainability

Hamburg proves that "greener" and "growing" are not mutually exclusive terms. Located 50 miles up the Elbe Estuary from the North Sea, Hamburg is Germany's second-largest city and Europe's third busiest port. At the same time, this city of 1.8 million people is pursuing an ambitious path to sustainability. Hamburg was named the 2011 European Green Capital for its green network, for its fight against climate change, and for transforming brownfields into innovative ecodistricts. By requiring and incentivizing significant reductions in green-house gas emissions, a public-private partnership here has also spawned a renewable energy sector that greatly benefits the regional economy.

The City's vision of Grunesnetz, or Green Network, began a century ago when Fritz Schumacher, the City's Chief Building Officer from 1909 to 1933, proposed a diverse system of neighborhood greenspace interconnected with greenways allowing residents access to larger parks and the countryside. The design concept resembles a web consisting of spokes radiating from a downtown lake and canal system at the confluence of the Elbe and Alster rivers. These radial spokes are linked by an inner ring created when the old city walls and fortifications were largely replaced by a system of gardens and parks, including Planten un Blomen, a botanical garden that offers a natural refuge in the heart of the City (Hamburg, undated; European Commission, 2011).

The Green Network reappeared in plan after plan during the 20th Century, reaffirming the idea of interlinked open spaces aimed at enabling people to move around the city or from the city to outlying forests using footpaths and cycle tracks undisturbed by road traffic and surrounded by greenery. On the Alsterwanderweg trail, which parallels the Alster River, cyclists and hikers travel by linked greenways from downtown to the reserves that largely dominate the northern end of Hamburg and now serve as a permanent home for numerous species. Hamburg considers the Green Network to be essential to the City's identity as well as its recreational, mobility and biodiversity goals. As a result, Hamburg is committed to an ongoing program of protecting the existing system and closing its remaining gaps (Hamburg, undated; European Commission, 2011).

Figure 3-1: *The Alsterwanderweg invites walking or biking from central Hamburg to the surrounding greenbelt.*

Figure 3-2: *The Alster Lakes add a blue dimension to a radial spoke in Hamburg's Green Network.*

The European Green Capital judges were also impressed with the sheer amount of greenspace in Hamburg. Almost 90 percent of all residents live within 300 meters of parkland, which largely explains why Hamburg's 1,460 parks experience over one million visitors every week. Hamburg's 31 nature reserves occupy roughly eight percent of Hamburg's total land area, the highest percentage in Germany. Hamburg places 19 percent of its land area within 36 landscape protection areas that conserve cultural and ecological resources as well as landscape features. In addition, Hamburg's ubiquitous lakes, rivers and canals are generally accessible to the public, including the 184-hectare Alster Lakes that provide habitat and an aquatic playground in the heart of the City (European Commission, 2009; European Commission, 2011; Hamburg, 2008; Hamburg, 2012).

Hamburg is growing its busy port while simultaneously restoring the health of the environmentally-significant Elbe Estuary. Although some Hamburg docks have become obsolete, the port still occupies ten percent of the City and harbor activity as a whole continues to grow. This is Europe's third-busiest port, handling 100 million tons of cargo annually and generating over 150,000 jobs. To reduce air pollution and greenhouse gas emissions, the port minimizes truck traffic in favor of rail transfer, making the Port of Hamburg the largest freight rail hub in Europe. The Port's shipping channel is the ecologically-important Elbe Estuary, a Natura 2000 site. Consequently, Hamburg and its partners have embarked on a unique contaminant-remediation program and created the 137-square kilometer Hamburg Wadden Sea National Park in the Elbe Estuary, now a UNESCO world heritage site, which preserves the largest mudflat on Earth and habitat for over 2,000 animal species (European Commission, 2011; Hamburg, 2008; Hamburg Port Authority, 2013).

Hamburg reduced per-capita CO_2 emissions over 25 percent between 1990 and 2005 by launching renewable energy projects, forming energy-saving partnerships with private industry and expanding its already-green transportation infrastructure. Almost all Hamburg residents live within 300 meters of high-frequency public transportation. For the last half century, a single transportation association has steadily built ridership by coordinating metro, bus and regional rail services. In 2011, the Hamburg Transportation

Association reported 691 million passengers, a 2.2 percent increase over the previous year (Berrini and Bono, 2010; Hamburg, 2008; Hamburg, 2012).

Although Hamburg is not as bicycle friendly as Copenhagen or Amsterdam, it nevertheless earns a place in the top 20 cities worldwide. Hamburg already had more than 1,700 kilometers of cycle lanes in 2008 when it adopted an ambitious strategy aimed at doubling bike traffic by expanding the network and improving safety. One year later, Hamburg launched StadtRAD, its bike share system that was logging over 2 million trips per year by 2012. Hamburg further motivates cycling by enforcing a 30 kilometer per hour speed limit on almost half of its street system (Hamburg, 2008; Union Cycliste Internationale, 2014).

Hamburg leads by example in reducing CO_2 emissions. The City cut energy use by 22 percent in 65,000 units of public housing and recycles or incinerates all municipal waste, fueling district heating and electrical generation systems rather than filling landfills. The City converted a contaminated landfill into Energy Hill, where wind turbines and solar collectors now provide electricity for 4,000 homes. Hamburg also transformed a World War II flak tower into Energy Bunker, which generates electricity with photovoltaics and warms 3,000 homes using a massive water reservoir heated by solar thermal, biomass, wood and waste heat from a nearby industrial plant. As an educational exhibit, complete with café, the Energy Bunker attracted almost 100,000 visitors in the first six months that it was open to the public (Dezeen, 2014; Hamburg, 2008; Hamburg 2012; Hamburg, 2016).

Since trade and industry produce roughly half of Hamburg's carbon emissions, the City has created various incentives for the private sector to reduce energy use and mitigate climate change. In 2003, the City and its partners launched the Eco-Partnership Project, which provides free consultation and the recognition of a Green Capital logo to firms that voluntarily commit to resource conservation measures surpassing standard requirements. When the 1000th firm joined the Eco-Partnership in 2015, Hamburg noted that competitiveness was motivating companies to join the partnership in addition to more conventional inducements. The Partnership also manages a Companies for Resource Protection program that provides financial support to private firms as well as technical advice. As of 2012, the energy-saving investments of this public-private effort was annually saving 163,700 tons of carbon emissions, 26,500 tons of waste and 712,300 cubic meters of water (European Commission, 2011; Hamburg, 2012; Hamburg, 2015).

Figure 3-3: *A public garden in Hamburg's inner green ring surrounding the downtown.*

Hamburg aims to contain sprawl by transforming obsolete industrial, port, rail, post office and military facilities into sustainable neighborhoods and ecodistricts. HafenCity, a former dock and industrial area, is adjacent to downtown and expands the city center by 40 percent. Served by a new metro line, this 155-hectare new town will accommodate 12,000 residents and 45,000 workers in energy-efficient buildings served by a district heating system fueled by renewable energy sources. Described as a "City of Plazas, Parks and Promenades", 23 percent of HafenCity is public open space with another 14 percent secured by public access rights. HafenCity is also the home of Hamburg's newest architectural icon, Elbe Philharmonic Hall, which perches atop an old warehouse and ranks as Hamburg's tallest occupied building (European Commission, 2011; Hamburg, 2008; Kreutz, 2010).

Using incentives and regulations to minimize waste, Hamburg is growing a robust green industrial sector. More than 600 renewable energy companies were located in and around Hamburg as of 2009. To further expand this exportable expertise, the City formed the Hamburg Renewable Energy Cluster in that year, networking private firms with institutions, universities and NGOs to inspire and support ongoing research and development. By 2011, two global manufacturers of wind turbines located in Hamburg and the Renewable Energy Cluster had grown to 163 companies, putting Hamburg on the map as a world center for alternative energy innovation (European Commission, 2011; Hamburg, 2012). By building a livable city with a green network that appeals to the creative class and responding to the challenges of a finite planet, Hamburg is demonstrating that leadership in sustainability can be a catalyst rather than a deterrent to economic prosperity.

CHAPTER 4

Vitoria-Gasteiz, Spain: Growing up – not out

Vitoria-Gasteiz is a walkable city and it aims to stay that way. This city of 242,000 people is the capital of the Basque Autonomous Community in northern Spain as well as the 2012 European Green Capital. Vitoria earned that prize by fighting climate change, building an eco-friendly transportation system and transforming abused land into an award-winning greenbelt. Many of these achievements are the result of a compact urban area where everything is close to everything else, including greenspace both within the city and in the surrounding countryside.

Even though Vitoria's population has tripled since the 1960s, 81 percent of its residents live within 1,500 meters of the city center. Not surprisingly, over half the trips here occur on foot. Despite that enviable statistic, Vitoria is building "super-blocks" – districts in which peripheral streets remain open to through traffic while interior streets are limited to pedestrians, bicyclists, deliveries and motorists who live in the super-block, all at a maximum speed limit of 10 kilometers per hour. This reconfiguration of the right of way converts 70 percent of the space previously reserved for cars into car-free public space. Vitoria has installed super-blocks in its downtown, including the Medieval Center with landmarks dating back to the 11th

Figure 4-1: *Super-block concepts were tested in Vitoria's Medieval Center.*

century. Eventually, the city plans to reduce "private vehicle primary streets" to 43 percent of the roadway network, which will make "pedestrian priority streets" the bulk of Vitoria's circulation system (European Commission, 2010; European Union, 2012; Vitoria-Gasteiz, 2010).

Vitoria promoted other eco-friendly transportation modes by building tram lines, improving bus service and adopting new parking regulations, changes which generated a 45 percent increase in public transportation ridership. In addition to a 33-kilometer network of pedestrian paths, Vitoria offers 97 kilometers of cycle lanes/paths in the urban area plus 91 kilometers of pedestrian/cycle paths in the greenbelt surrounding the urban area. As a result, a bicyclist can reach any destination within the urban area in 15 minutes or less (European Union, 2012; Vitoria-Gasteiz, 2010).

Compact development is essential to these accomplishments. Vitoria's urban area comprises less than 15 percent of the total land area of the municipality but accommodates 98 percent of the total population. From 2001 to 2010, the city maintained that ratio, capturing 97 percent of the municipality's total growth within the greenbelt by redeveloping underutilized properties at densities of up to 400 dwelling units per hectare. In the two neighborhoods adjacent to 247-acre Salburua Park, the city introduced a policy known as re-densification calling for increases in the densities previously found in the general plan. Although re-densification proposals initially generate tension within neighborhoods, the city has found that residents ultimately learn that these actions improve local commercial activity, safety, public services and urban amenities, such as the ability to stroll through an adjacent natural area like Salburua to see the ducks and deer (Vitoria-Gasteiz, 2010).

Revitalization of obsolete buildings and contaminated land also helps Vitoria maintain its high density. Between 2001 and 2010, the city reduced its inventory of derelict property by 500 hectares, mostly by remediating and reusing brownfields and vacant industrial buildings. Historic rehabilitation also plays an important role, such as the multi-million-euro restoration of an 800-year-old cathedral and surrounding residential landmarks in the Medieval Center. These efforts to grow up rather than out have resulted in an overall density of over 67 inhabitants per hectare in the urban area and puts 90 percent of the population within 300 meters of basic services

(European Union, 2012; Vitoria-Gasteiz, 2010).

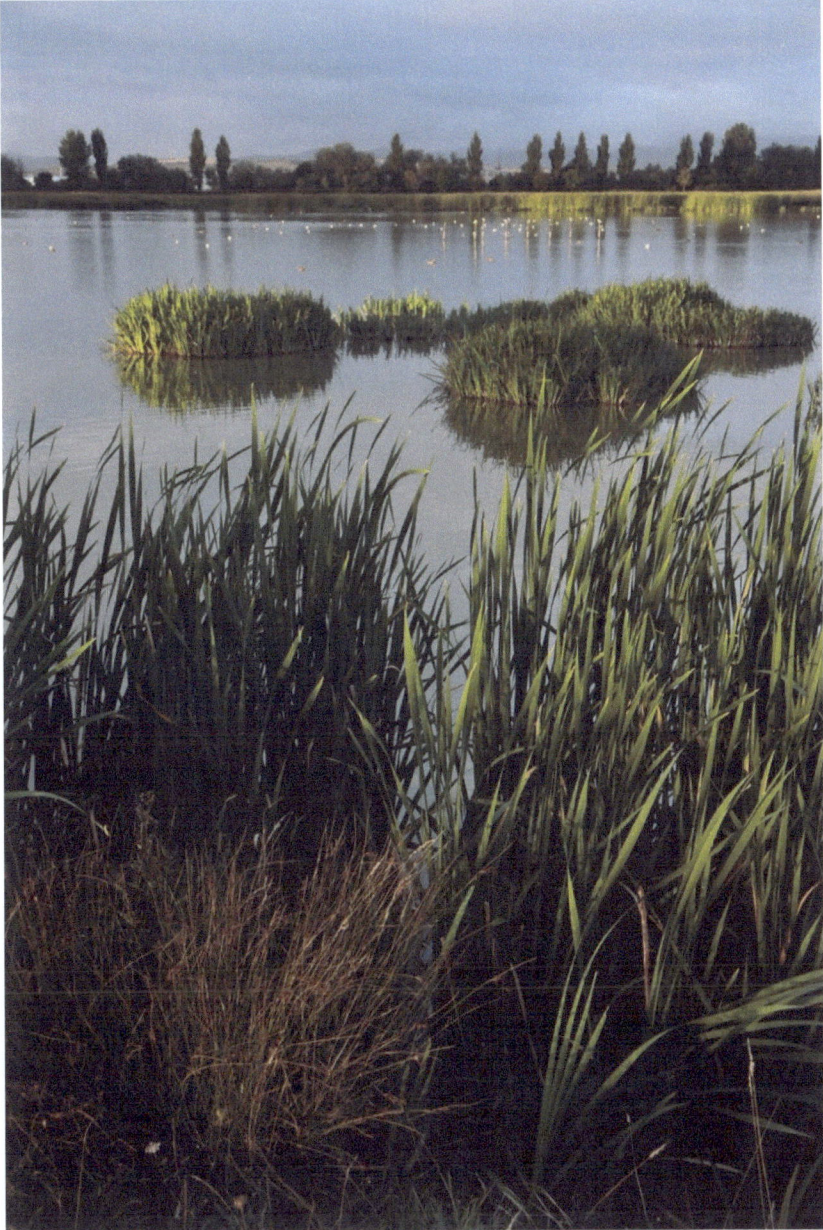

Figure 4-2: *Vitoria-Gasteiz created its greenbelt by restoring abandoned gravel pits, garbage dumps and the Salburua Wetlands shown here.*

Vitoria residents are also close to greenery. To be exact, the entire population lives within 300 meters of public open space. These parks and gardens are interconnected and link to the city's award-wining greenbelt, a string of five large parks that encircle the urban area, forming an unofficial urban growth boundary. The greenbelt features 91 kilometers of pedestrian/bicycle paths for those who want to wander for an hour as well as those who prefer to completely circumnavigate the urban area. Vitoria's local planning think tank, the Environmental Studies Centre, refers to the greenbelt as an "eco-recreational corridor" (Environmental Studies Centre, 2012; European Union, 2012; Vitoria-Gasteiz, 2016).

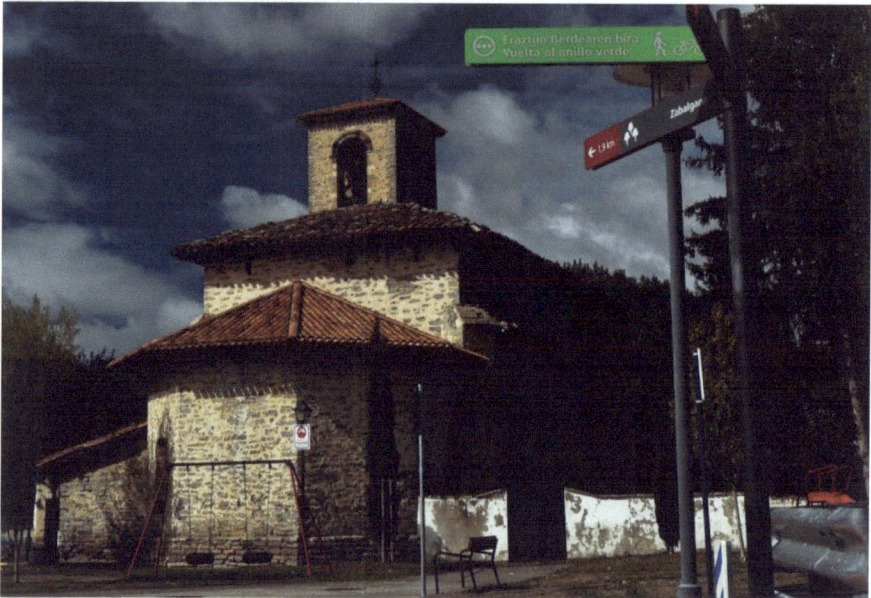

Figure 4-3: *This historic church serves as a rest stop for walkers and bicyclists on the 91-kilometer network of pedestrian/cycle paths within the greenbelt encircling Vitoria.*

The greenbelt parks were former gravel pits, burned areas, garbage dumps and other degraded land that Vitoria began reclaiming in 1992 for multiple benefits including ecology, water management, alternative transportation and biodiversity as well as recreation. The

Zadorra River, which forms the northern segment of the greenbelt, was redesigned to retain storm water, create habitat and improve stream water quality, ultimately becoming a Natura 2000 site. The previously-disturbed Salburua Wetlands, located at the eastern end of the greenbelt, underwent a hydrological/vegetative makeover and is now home to numerous endangered species including the European mink, one of the most threatened carnivores on Earth. Today, birds literally flock to Salburua, which has been listed as a Natura 2000 site and an internationally-significant Ramsar wetland (Environmental Studies Center, 2012; European Union, 2012; O'Neill & Rudden, 2010; Vitoria-Gasteiz, 2016).

Vitoria's Environmental Studies Centre sees the city's urban green infrastructure as a series of concentric circles. The parks and gardens around the city center, or interior green belt, link to the larger greenbelt encircling the entire urban area. Beyond that lies an agricultural belt covering 58 percent of the city's total land area. This area has been environmentally degraded by industrialized farming and the removal of hedgerows, riversides and woods. However, the good news is that this belt is still largely undeveloped and the Centre proposes a restoration process that includes the conservation and improvement of natural vegetation as well as the promotion of organic and ecological farming practices that respect native plants, streams and aquifers.

Revitalization of the agricultural belt would improve fertility and the quality of the rural landscape while restoring environmental linkages to the outermost green circle formed by the forested mountains that largely define the municipality's borders. These forests are well-protected by public ownership and ancient rules governing the use of natural resources such as water and pasturage. As a result, native species make up 91 percent of the forest (Environmental Studies Centre, 2012; European Union, 2012; Vitoria-Gasteiz, 2010).

Building on its accomplishments, Vitoria has committed to aggressive goals for the future. The city aims to continue its fight against climate change by expanding its bicycle infrastructure, superblocks and other eco-friendly transportation options while increasing its already impressive achievements in alternative energy generation with a target of eventually becoming carbon neutral. The city also pledges to retain its compact form, improve the bio-capacity of the urban area and incorporate biodiversity as a structural element in street design. In its quest for connectivity, Vitoria will expand the greenbelt even further and improve ecological linkages within the entire municipality and beyond: "Connecting it with the mountains surrounding the city will provide Vitoria-Gasteiz with a new ecological dimension, linking the city with the natural spaces known as the Highland Belt, and making it part of the great pan-European ecological corridor that runs from the Galician mountains to the Alps" (European Union, 2012, p51).

CHAPTER 5

Nantes, France: City of eco-neighborhoods

Nantes' past, present and future are built on water. Located on the Loire River roughly 30 miles from the Atlantic Ocean, Nantes was historically a harbor city. But in the 1980s, shipbuilding and many other port-related industries began moving away, forcing Nantes to reinvent itself. This renaissance is being successfully accomplished by curbing sprawl and concentrating new growth in the city center, often in ecodistricts that showcase energy conservation and resource efficiency. While increasing density, Nantes is simultaneously growing a livable environment for humans and other species using a green and blue network that provides habitat, open space, waterside walks and non-motorized transportation routes largely alongside the City's numerous streams and rivers (European Commission, 2016).

Nantes' green roots predate the French Revolution. During the reign of King Louis XIV, ship captains brought plants from around the world to Nantes, where they were cultivated before moving to the Royal Gardens in Paris. This practice nurtured horticultural expertise that is still evident today in Nantes' many gardens, including the Jardin des Plantes, established in 1806 and now home to 11,000 species and varieties (Nantes, 2010). Today, Nantes maintains an urban forest of 100,000 trees as well as a network of parks, gardens and other open space that places every resident within 300 meters of greenspace (Nantes, 2014; Nantes, O'Neill & Rudden, 2010).

Figure 5-1: *The entire population of Nantes lives within 300 meters of greenspace, including the grounds of the Chateau des ducs de Bretagne.*

The Loire and several other rivers and streams meander through Nantes, forming over 250 kilometers of major watercourses and 9,500 hectares of wetlands (O'Neill & Rudden, 2010). Almost 13 percent of Nantes is protected within four Natura 2000 sites including the banks of the Loire and Sevre rivers. The City and 23 surrounding communities, known as Nantes Metropole, are restoring these areas and revitalizing habitat for endangered species. Within its network of protected land and water, known as the green and blue framework, Nantes offers 210 kilometers of "waterside walks" aimed at using "multimodal green transport" to connect the public with nature (Nantes, 2010; European Commission, 2016).

In addition to waterside walks, Nantes' "Soft Mobility Plan" aims to significantly increase the percentage of trips taken by bicycle (European Commission, 2016). In response, Nantes expanded its bikeway system to 470 kilometers of cycle paths or tracks and established a bikeshare system offering almost 800 bicycles at 89 stations (Nantes, 2014). Bike commuters and recreational cyclists can also use a 365-km trail that largely follows the tow path of the Nantes-Brest Canal. Another bike path on the banks of the Loire River is part of the 3,653-km EuroVelo Rivers Route connecting Nantes with Romania by way of nine separate countries (Nantes, 2010). In 2009, Nantes won the Civitas City of the Year Award for cycle and public transportation improvements as well as pedestrianizing streets within the city center (O'Neill and Rudden, 2010).

Nantes has also been a leader in public transportation. In 1985, Nantes became the first city in France to successfully reintroduce a modern tram line. By 2014, that tram line was carrying 120,000 passengers daily, making it the third busiest line in the country, and Nantes now has three additional tram lines, commuter rail, water buses and a busway. By 2009, 95 percent of Nantes' population lived within 300 meters of public transportation with hourly or better service (European Commission, 2010; Nantes, 2010; Nantes, 2014). These ecomobility strategies are a key component of Nantes' Climate Action Plan, which aims to reduce CO_2 emissions by 25 percent between 1990 and 2025.

Figure 5-2: *Green transport on a "waterside walk" along the Erdre River.*

Roughly 61 percent of Nantes Metropole is in nature or agriculture and the population is projected to grow by almost 17 percent to 700,000 in 2030 (European Commission, 2016). There are few physical barriers to keep growth from spilling into the picturesque countryside. But Nantes' land use plan aims to block sprawl by concentrating growth within currently developed areas, particularly within the transportation-rich central city and on brownfield sites. Nantes also wants these redevelopment areas to be models of sustainability and nature-friendliness (Nantes, 2010).

Ecodistrict Ile de Nantes is a five-kilometer-long island in the Loire River that formerly housed a foundry, ship building yard and other port-related industries. A 20-year redevelopment project is transforming this island into a model mixed-use neighborhood with worksites, retail and civic space as well as residences. Its renewable energy credentials include a district heating network fueled by waste and wood, solar thermal installations, photovoltaics and an aerothermal heat pump (Hure, 2013). Some of the former industrial structures here have been repurposed as landscape architecture, including the Foundries Garden, which houses 200 trees and 100 plant varieties within the girders and furnaces once used to forge propellers. The former shipyards are now the home of Island Machines, a truly unique enterprise that builds whimsical animated artworks including a mechanical elephant that lumbers around the island carrying more than a dozen passengers on its back (Nantes, 2010).

Nantes is also justifiably proud of its Bottiere-Chenaie Eco-Neighborhood, a pedestrian-friendly development that achieves densities of up to 120 units per hectare yet incorporates open space elements that allow close contact with nature and, of course, water. Nantes employs pesticide-free management of greenspace in Bottiere-Chenaie and throughout the city in order to generally improve environmental health and, more specifically, to sustain the bee populations that that are critical to the City's beloved trees and gardens. In fact, Nantes uses bee vitality as a measure of overall ecosystem quality. The City is home to almost 90 beekeepers and apiaries are located in parks and atop buildings throughout the city center, including the roof of the Opera House (Nantes, 2010).

Figure 5-3: *Young equestrians in La Chezine River Park, a finger of Nantes' green and blue framework.*

Nantes' accomplishments have not gone unnoticed. In 2009, Nantes won the Eco-cities prize from the French Ministry of Sustainable Development using the submission theme: "To build the city around the River". France also awarded the eco-neighborhood title to three projects in Nantes out of a total of 28 eco-neighborhoods in the entire country (Nantes, 2010).

At the international level, the European Commission named Nantes the 2013 European Green Capital. In addition to the physical achievements mentioned above, the European Green Capital jurors were impressed with Nantes' understanding of the need to mold the behavior of individual citizens. The Nantes Exhibition Centre hosts learning experiences like "my life – my town – my planet" which motivates school-age children to make the connection between their actions and the health of Mother Earth. But Nantes also takes its sustainability message on the road, using impossible-to-ignore attractions like the Flying Greenhouse, Island Machine's fanciful 53-foot tall spaceship powered by on-board composting.

Green is also good for Nantes economy. In 2013 alone, Nantes hosted 8,400 delegates to over 20 international events on sustainability issues including the World Mayor's Summit on Climate Change and the Ecocity World Summit. During the Ecocity Summit, the Feeding of the 5,000 offered a culinary protest against food waste with a feast prepared from "ugly" fruits and vegetables that ordinarily are thrown out because of harmless imperfections (Nantes, 2014). In the process of sharing its experiences, Nantes is clearly building its international reputation while pursuing its economic development and eco-tourism strategies.

CHAPTER 6

Copenhagen, Denmark: Good cycle karma

To "Copenhagenize" means to design cities for bikes rather than cars. Not surprisingly, Copenhagen sits atop the Copenhagenize Index, an international measure of a city's bike friendliness. But the accomplishments of this city of 562,379 people goes well beyond bicycles. Copenhagen also showcases car-free zones, a sprawl-curbing green structure, swimmable harbor water and a climate action plan aimed at making this city the world's first carbon neutral capital by 2025. The innovations and investments needed to achieve its ambitious goals energize an economic development strategy which is making the "green sector" a significant engine of regional growth. Often appearing at or near the top of various quality-of-life indices, Copenhagen also demonstrates the positive link between sustainability and livability.

In its 2007 Eco-Metropolis Plan, Copenhagen aimed to become the "World's Best City for Cyclists" by 2015. According to many experts, including the Union Cycliste Internationale, Copenhagen achieved that goal ahead of schedule. By 2014, 62 percent of all Copenhageners biked to work. This remarkable mode share is made possible by 346 kilometers of separated bike lanes, 23 kilometers of other bike lanes and 42 kilometers of green cycle lanes, which are generally through parks or otherwise located away from busy streets (Copenhagen, 2007; Copenhagen, 2011; Copenhagen, 2013; Copenhagen, 2015; UCI, 2014).

Although Copenhagen had a robust bicycling culture in the first half of the 20th Century, the automobile threatened to take over the City in the 1960s. During this decade, some bike lanes were removed in an ill-conceived attempt to facilitate automobile use. But in the 1970s and 1980s, Copenhagen executed a U-turn thanks to rising oil prices and a realization that trying to accommodate cars only invites more to come. Car lanes and parking were converted to cycle tracks, which now parallel every major roadway. All other streets are restricted to speed limits of 30 kilometers per hour (19 mph) or, in some cases, 15 kilometers per hour (9 mph), and bikes are welcome on public transportation. As a result, Copenhageners can safely, quickly and healthily commute "door-to-door" by bike. In an effort to get everyone on bikes, Copenhagen widens existing cycle tracks, removes snow from cycle lanes first, gives bikes a head start at traffic signals and times traffic signals to match cycling speeds so that bicyclists can ride a "green wave" through the City. In addition to infrastructure, Copenhagen promotes the cycling habit using events and campaigns such as "good cycle karma" which rewards cyclists with free chocolate (Copenhagen, 2011; Copenhagen, 2013; Gehl, 2010).

Copenhagen has pioneered the conversion of streets to car-free zones. This process began in 1962, when Copenhagen removed cars from a one-kilometer stretch of Stroget Street. Proving the skeptics wrong, Stroget attracted significantly more pedestrians, creating what is now a thriving shopping district. Encouraged by this success, Copenhagen has since increased its car-free zones sevenfold. Copenhagen is also fortunate to be the home base for urban designers who have spent decades analyzing and advocating for streetscapes that attract and engage people using human scale, interesting facades, soft edges and many other techniques that are now part of every planner's playbook. Starting with the City's first "public space – public life" study in 1968, the approaches demonstrated in Copenhagen have been adopted in many cities around the world including Melbourne and New York City (Gehl, 2010).

Figure 6-1: *Stroget, car-free since 1962, was the first of Copenhagen's many pedestrianized streets.*

Green areas cover 25 percent of Copenhagen and lie within 300 meters of 80 percent of all residents. These City open spaces are integral to a regional plan that concentrates development within urban corridors, or fingers, separated by rural land, or green wedges. This concept was first envisioned in 1928 and informally guided successive regional plans throughout the 20th Century. At first, most of the green wedges consisted of ordinary agricultural landscapes, making them vulnerable to sprawl since they had little official protection. But Copenhagen and its neighboring jurisdictions began transforming this farmland into parks, forests, athletic fields, community gardens, golf courses and landscape protection areas. Through these efforts, average citizens likely realized the value of these areas and the green wedges were formally adopted by the Denmark Planning Act of 2007 (Copenhagen, 2011; Veire, Petersen and Henchel, undated).

Figure 6-2: More than half of all Copenhageners commute to work by bicycle.

Protection of the green wedges provides the continuous habitat needed for wildlife to thrive. Copenhagen's strategy for biodiversity, "Room for Nature", also recognizes that preservation of parks and natural areas helps the city adapt to the growing threats posed by climate change, such as a projection that the storm water sewer system will not be capable of accommodating 30 percent of the run-off generated by future cloudbursts. In addition to physical solutions, Copenhagen aims to grow nature awareness, particularly in young people. The City runs a Nature Workshop attracting up to 10,000 visitors each year and offers a Nature Detectives game at several playgrounds which engages children in environmental education activities (Copenhagen, 2011; O'Neill and Rudden, 2012).

"A Green and Blue Capital City", one of the Eco-metropolis Plan's four themes, challenges Copenhagen to protect water quality as well as greenspace. In response, the City has accomplished costly water quality restoration projects. This investment has paid off by restoring the aquatic environment, renewing the vitality of waterfront-adjacent neighborhoods, and generally improving the quality of life for the City as a whole. Rather than travel to distance beaches, Copenhageners can now take a dip in any of the three seawater pools in Copenhagen harbor (Copenhagen, 2011; Copenhagen, 2012).

Copenhagen wants to accommodate a growing population and economy as close to the City Center as possible. To concentrate development, former industrial, military, port, and rail facilities are being remediated and converted to residential/commercial districts. The Orestad neighborhood, a portion of which was previously military property, lies only ten minutes from downtown and now features a new metro rail line as well as several high-tech buildings including the Copenhagen Concert Hall. Orestad incorporates lots of open space, a preserved meadow and a storm water management system called SUDS. The Sustainable Urban Drainage System, or SUDS, locally treats runoff from roadways before adding it to rooftop discharge and releasing both to the meandering canals that add recreational options for residents and complement Orestad's overall design (Copenhagen, 2011; Copenhagen, 2012; European Commission, 2012b).

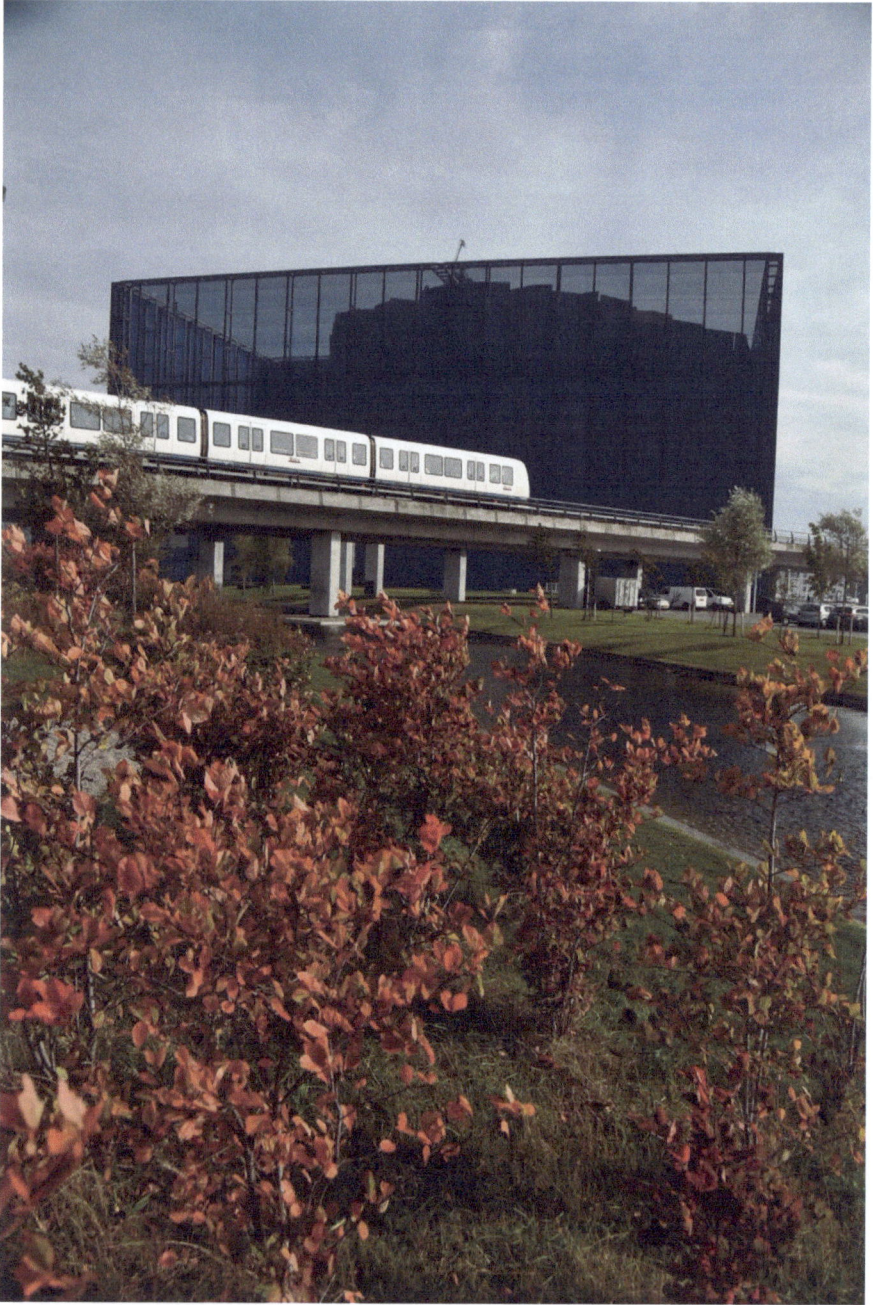

Figure 6-3: *Orestad features the Copenhagen Concert Hall, a new metro rail line and recreational canals supplemented by locally-treated storm water.*

Copenhagen is a leader in fighting climate change. Between 1995 and 2012, the City cut carbon emissions a remarkable 40 percent. Much of this reduction resulted from switching from coal to biomass in the combined heating and power districts that serve 98 percent of all households in the City. In less than ten years, Copenhagen aims to be a net exporter of power from a biomass and wind-based system. To meet that goal, the City plans to add 30,000 square meters of photovoltaic panels on municipal buildings and erect 100 wind turbines with a combined capacity of 360 MW. With this aggressive strategy, Copenhagen has challenged itself to become the world's first carbon neutral capital by 2025. Given the City's past track record and approved funding plan, experts believe that Copenhagen will hit that target (European Commission, 2012b; European Commission, 2014; O'Neill and Rudden, 2012).

Copenhagen has not just survived but thrived on its carbon diet. Between 2005 and 2014, City population rose by 15 percent and its economy grew by 18 percent while its carbon emissions fell by 31 percent. In 2010, the Danish wind industry employed 25,000 workers and was growing by 30 percent every year. The green sector as a whole in the Copenhagen Region grew 55 percent between 2005 and 2009 and is now seen as an important wealth generator and economic engine. Public-private partnerships have formed to help firms profit from this momentum, including Green Businesses, a network of almost 1,000 companies working on noise reduction, air pollution and water contamination as well as fossil fuel consumption (Copenhagen, 2011; Copenhagen, 2015).

Although famous for bicycling and alternative energy, Copenhagen pursues every facet of sustainability. The City won the 2014 European Green Capital Award for an integrated vision that tackles economic and social issues as well as environmental concerns (European Commission, 2012a). The expert judges for this award gave Copenhagen high marks in every category and noted that the City is repeatedly recognized for its high quality of life. The judges also highlighted the role of public-private partnerships in using eco-innovations as an economic development strategy and praised Copenhagen as "…an excellent role model in terms of urban planning and design to cities across Europe and the world" (European Commission, 2012a, p4; European Commission, 2012b).

CHAPTER 7

Bristol, United Kingdom: Incubating change

Bristol describes itself as a "Laboratory for Change". In awarding the 2015 title of European Green Capital to this city of 441,000 in South West England, the judges highlighted Bristol's accomplishments in energy performance, transportation and sustainable land use, particularly the redevelopment of contaminated sites in the city center and the coordination of its greenspace for active travel and wildlife preservation as well as recreation (European Commission, 2013).

As proof of its change-agent claim, Bristol became the UK pilot for ICLEI's Cities for Climate Protection program in 2000. The emission targets adopted by the City in 2004 were among the most ambitious in the UK. In 2009, the City surpassed the targets established by the EU and UK, calling for a 40 percent reduction by 2020 and an 80 percent reduction by 2050 using a 2005 baseline. True to that commitment, Bristol lowered its emissions 19 percent between 2005 and 2010 and now has the lowest CO_2 emissions per capita of all major UK cities (Bristol, 2012).

In 2013, Bristol installed wind-generating turbines on a former oil tank site, creating the first council-owned wind farm in the United Kingdom (Bristol, 2013). Leading by example, Bristol became the first UK city to fuel its boilers with wood waste from its parks and street trees. The City also motivates its citizens to adopt energy-saving lifestyles using its eco-home to demonstrate sustainability features and hosting a program called Bristol Green Doors which encourages people to tour retrofitted homes to see energy efficiency upgrades (Bristol, 2012).

In 2011, Bristol adopted building policies aimed at decreasing carbon emissions including a requirement that all new development install on-site renewable energy sources capable of achieving CO_2 emission goals that exceed UK standards by 20 percent. The UK Environment Agency headquarters here was the UK's most energy-efficient building in 2009. Similarly, the Southmead Hospital in Bristol is the UK's most energy efficient major hospital (Bristol, 2012). The Bristol development named CO_2 Zero was the first private residential development and the first live-work development in the UK to achieve Code Level 5, a near-zero standard for heating, light and ventilation (United Kingdom, 2009).

Figure 7-1: *Harborside is a successful redevelopment of the City's former docklands.*

Figure 7-2: *In addition to being the City's most famous structure, the Clifton Suspension Bridge is also a key link between central Bristol and its green belt.*

Bristol is commtted to concentrating new development in central areas. In the first decade of the 21st Century, 98 percent of business development and 94 percent of residential development occurred on brownfield sites. In 2007, the City adopted a policy of steering all development away from greenfield sites and into brownfields. The Harborside project transformed 26 hectares of contaminated city center land into a high density, mixed use neighborhood with walkways, cycle paths, waterfront access and vibrant public spaces including an amphitheater and Millennium Square, now the City's central plaza. Barton Hill, another inner city redevelopment project, reestablished the historic street pattern and created a neighborhood preferred by social housing tenants. Bristol is also redeveloping 80 hectares of industrial land near the central rail station into the Temple Quarter Enterprise Zone geared to attracting digital and low-carbon companies (Bristol, 2012).

By building entirely on brownfield sites, Bristol aims to keep sprawl out of the surrounding countryside. Bristol and its neighboring communities cooperate though the West of England Partnership to focus growth in existing centers and brownfields using strategic investments in housing, transportation, green infrastructure and maintenance of a sprawl-limited Green Belt. The region's Strategic Green Infrastructure Framework aims to protect rivers, wildlife corridors and parks that cross jurisdictional borders. (Bristol, 2012).

In addition to concentrating development, Bristol reduces transportation emissions by improving public transportation and providing non-motorized travel options. Bristol became the official demonstration Cycling City of the UK and invested 20 million pounds in cycling improvements between 2009 and 2011. There are now 299 kilometers of cycle lanes of which 131 kilometers are physically separated bikeways and bike paths (Bristol, 2012).

In 1977, Bristol citizens formed the group now known as Sustrans, a non-profit organization promoting sustainable transportation throughout the United Kingdom. In 1982, Sustrans led the construction of a 13-mile rail trail between Bristol and Bath which now links with a 45-mile path through the Forest of Avon around Bristol. The Bristol and Bath Railway Path has become the most popular trail in the country, transporting more people than the trains that formerly ran here. Today, Sustrans is coordinating development of the National Cycle Network, a system of cycle paths and routes that is already located within two miles of 75 percent of all people in the UK (Sustrans, 2016).

About one sixth of the City is subject to a pilot program limiting vehicles to 20 miles per hour in an effort to promote biking and walking. Based on the success of this demonstration project, the City plans to apply the 20 mph speed limit to all residential neighborhoods. Between 2004 and 2012, cycling increased 80 percent with impressive growth in commuting, female cyclists and trips within the city center as well as the 20 mph pilot zones (Bristol, 2012).

Over three quarters of Bristol residents live within 300 meters of bus, rail or other forms of public transportation. A zero-emission hydrogen waterbus is now under development with funding from the Bristol City Council. Bristol is also closing or removing roads in the city center to create civic and recreational features. As a prominent example, the City removed roadways that previously bisected Queens Square, creating a public park with pedestrian and cycle paths (Bristol, 2012).

Figure 7-3: *The 850-acre Ashton Court Estate Park offers ample space for recreation and nature.*

Almost one third of Bristol's total land area is blue or greenspace including 1,600 hectares of public parkland. Furthermore, more than 87 percent of Bristolians live within 300 meters of parks or other greenspace The Frome and Avon rivers meander through the City Center before passing through the Avon Gorge and flowing into the Severn Estuary. In 2011, the City added 80 hectares to the public park system with the acquisition of Stoke Park Estate. On the southern city limits, the Ashton Court Estate is the third busiest country park in the UK, offering 850 acres for all outdoor activities including a deer park. The historic, cycle/pedestrian-friendly Clifton Suspension Bridge over the Avon Gorge connects this mammoth park with the center of Bristol (Bristol, 2012).

The Bristol Wildlife Network, which applies to 27 percent of the city, protects habitats and natural corridors in new private developments as well as public projects. This network incorporates inner city segments of the Floating Harbor, originally a bypass of the Avon River controlled by locks to isolate docks from tidal-generated water level fluctuations. The wildlife network also includes several city parks including Greville Smyth Park and Brunel Open Space. The Severn Estuary, which provides habitat for birds of European importance, lies partly within the northern city boundaries and has been classified as a European Marine Site, Special Protection Area, Ramsar site and a Special Area of Conservation. The Avon Gorge is home to 27 species listed nationally as rare and threatened (Bristol, 2012).

Bristol pioneered urban wildlife protection in the UK, creating habitat in Brandon Hill Park in the city center in the 1980s and preserving Royate Hill as a Local Nature Reserve in the 1990s. More recent accomplishments include the protection of Troopers Hill and the designation of Grove Wood as a Town Village Green. Floating reed beds were recently introduced to the site of the city center's former industrial docks and otters have since returned to this area (Bristol, 2012).

In 2008, the City adopted the Bristol Biodiversity Action Plan which has been recognized as a model by the UK Government. In an effort to put people and habitat close to one another, the City adopted a goal of establishing 16 Local Nature Reserves by 2016

(Bristol, 2012).

Bristol uses renewable energy generated by its sludge biogas digesters to power the entire wastewater treatment plant. All of the sludge produced at the plant is used as soil amendments on local farmland. A triathlon, complete with swimming competition, is held annually in Bristol's floating harbor, one indication that the wastewater treatment system is effective as well as energy efficient (Bristol, 2012).

Bristol's green brand has been good for business. Sustainability and a high quality of life have succeeded in attracting high tech industries and a highly-educated work force as well as leading environmental organizations like City Farms, Forum for the Future, the Schumacher Institute and the national headquarters of the Environment Agency (Sawday, 2012). As a result, Bristol is incubating prosperity as well as change.

CHAPTER 8

Ljubljana, Slovenia: River as centerpiece

Ljubljana, home to 283,000 people, is the capital of Slovenia, the mountainous republic surrounded by Italy, Austria, Hungary and Croatia. After years of car-centric planning in the 20th Century, Ljubljana shifted to a more nature-friendly course, transforming the city center into an ecological zone, revitalizing its riverfront, redeveloping brownfields and protecting green areas, which form almost three-quarters of the City. In a major step toward connecting its protected landscapes to each other and to the city center, Ljubljana converted the perimeter fence that encircled the City during World War II into a 33-kilometer bike/walk trail that welcomes 30,000 citizens each year to a recreational march commemorating the City's liberation.

Figure 8-1: *The grounds of Ljubljana Castle form a green corridor linking the city center with the City's greenbelt across the Ljubljanica River.*

Ljubljana is bordered to the north by forested mountains and to the south by the lowland fields and marshes surrounding the Ljubljanica River. The heart of Ljubljana is linked to this greenbelt by riparian corridors and green wedges, including a three-park complex that extends to the western edge of downtown and a wooded ridge that connects the City's eastern hinterlands to the open space encircling Ljubljana Castle above the historic city center (Treanor, Connolly and McEvoy, 2014). As a result, Ljubljana not only offers more than 540 square meters of public greenspace per person but puts almost all of its residential areas within 300 meters of public greenspace (Ljubljana, 2013).

Greenspace constitutes almost three quarters of Ljubljana, with over 16 percent of the City's total land area in Natura 2000 sites (EGC, 2014). More than 20 percent of the City has some form of nature protection status including special-purpose forests and ecological areas as well as Natura 2000 sites. Tivoli-Roznik-Sisenski Landscape Park protects habitat for endangered species at the doorstep of downtown Ljubljana, allowing over 1.7 million visitors per year to get in touch with nature. At 135 square kilometers, Ljubljansko Barje, the largest of Ljubljana's four landscape parks, protects natural riparian forests and wetlands while incorporating farming techniques that maintain a high level of biodiversity (Ljubljana, 2013).

Ljubljana is committed to compact development, primarily on infill and brownfield sites including disused industrial zones, abandoned military facilities, remediated waste dumps and illegal settlements. Specifically, more than 80 percent of the areas designated for development require the regeneration and renewal of degraded land. Between 2001 and 2013, Ljubljana transformed brownfields into five parks and nine residential complexes with over 1,200 new dwelling units. Ljubljana and its private-sector partners are currently redeveloping a 228-hectare industrial area into a model ecodistrict incorporating sustainable building technologies and featuring a "central park" with green corridor linkages to the downtown ecological district (Ljubljana, 2013).

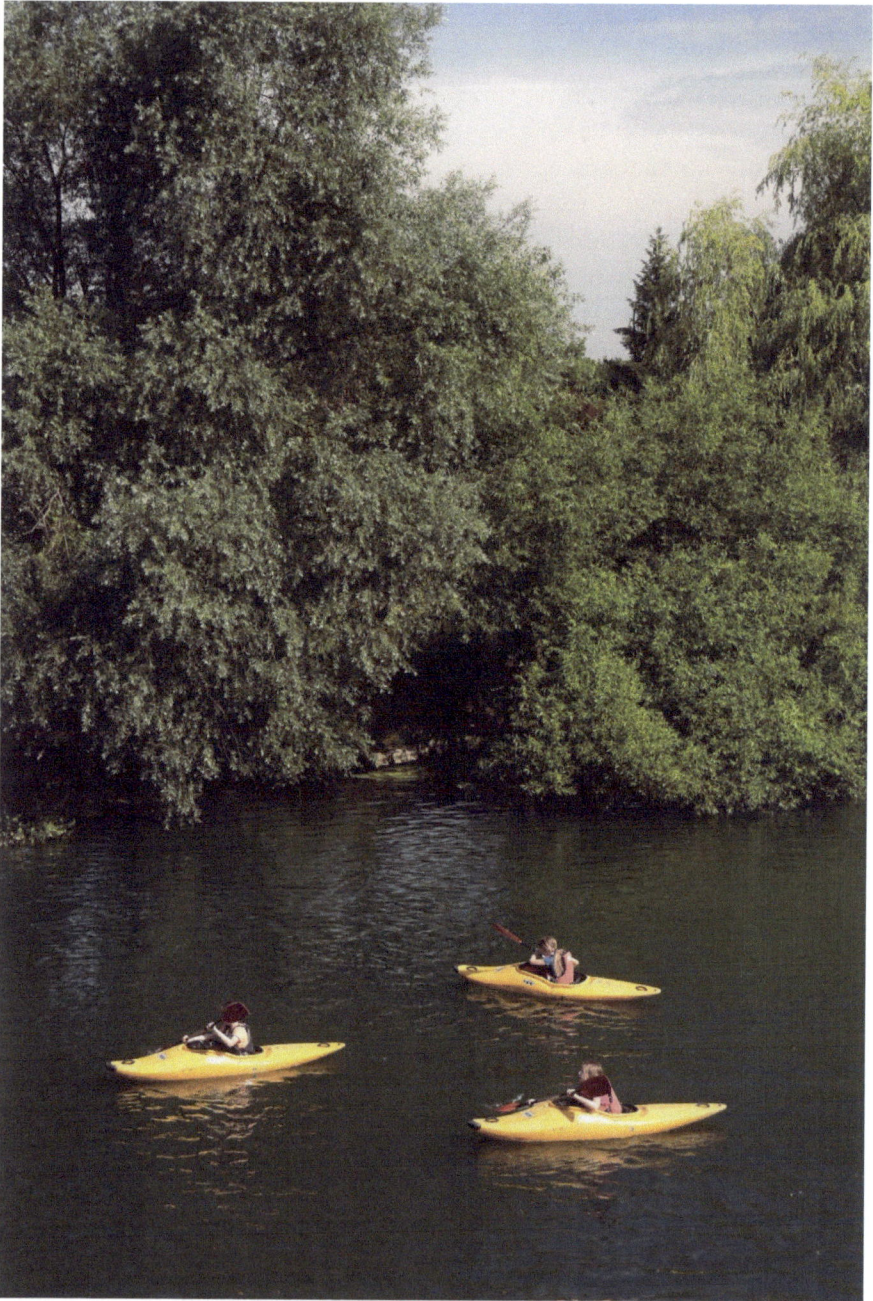

Figure 8-2: *The entire Ljubljanica River is protected by Natura 2000 status over the roughly 15 miles that it meanders through the City.*

The renovation of the Ljubljanica River restored and interconnected an iconic riparian environment through a part of downtown that had been degraded by traffic and parking. This project included the construction of paths along the river and four new bridges for bicyclists and pedestrians, improvements that extended the downtown ecological zone and created public spaces allowing people to reach as well as cross the water. These interventions earned the 2012 European Prize for Urban Public Space and restored the riverfront to its former glory as the City's preeminent public space (Ljubljana, 2013; Bordas, 2012).

In 2007, Ljubljana declared its city center as an ecological zone closed to motor vehicles with the exception of early-morning deliveries. Over the five-year period ending in 2013, the City expanded the public space reserved for pedestrians and bicyclists to more than 30 streets, a 550-percent increase. In addition to the obvious benefits of safety, air quality and reduction of greenhouse gas emissions, establishment of the ecological zone has reduced noise levels by almost 6dB(A), creating a large, peaceful place in the heart of the City (O'Neill and MacHugh, 2013).

Ljubljana has greatly improved public transport reliability by rebuilding its major downtown arterial street exclusively for buses and bikes. The City's bike share system, with 30 docking stations, is also attracting widespread use. As a result, Ljubljana has substantially reduced automobile use and aims for a 2020 future in which the three mobility categories (cars, public transport and non-motorized travel) will each account for one third of all trips. These eco-mobility efforts, coupled with plans for compact growth and energy conservation, have prompted Ljubljana to target a 50- to 80-percent reduction in greenhouse gas emissions between 2008 and 2050 (EGC, 2014).

In addition to the outlying greenbelt, Ljubljana has created an inner green ring by retooling the strip of land that encircled the City during World War II where barbed wire fences and guard towers literally separated Ljubljana from its surrounding countryside for over three years. When the City was liberated on May 9, 1945, the citizens used this former no-mans-land to build a path which is now used for a memorial walk held every year on May 9 attended by more than 30,000 people. Over the years, the City and its volunteers planted 7,400 trees on what is now a 33-kilometer recreational trail known as the Path of Remembrance and Comradeship. The path is used by walkers, joggers and bicyclists for exercise and recreation. In addition, it provides a non-motorized way for residents to reach many of the City's major destinations including the zoo, the Ljubljana Architectural Museum, Fuzine Castle and several green areas (Valentine, 2010).

Figure 8-3: *Ljubljana replaced the military barrier that encircled the City during WW Two with the 35-kilometer recreational trail called the Path of Remembrance and Comradeship.*

Ljubljana is succeeding in becoming a greener city by restoring its natural environment, concentrating development on remediated brownfields and changing a traffic-bound downtown into a largely car-free pedestrian zone. These accomplishments have not gone unnoticed. The European Commission named Ljubljana the 2016 European Green Capital and the City has won international recognition for sustainable tourism. In addition to its inherent benefits, this nature-friendly transformation has boosted tourism here. Between 2002 and 2014, Ljubljana has seen tourist visits more than double (Ljubljana Tourism, 2016).

CHAPTER 9

Essen, Germany: Greening brownfields

E ssen lies at the heart of the Ruhr Valley, at one time one of the world's largest concentrations of the coal and steel industries. Since the mid-20th Century, this city of 574,000 people in southwestern Germany has been transforming its previously-degraded landscape into a green city largely by sustainably redeveloping disused land and by restoring over half of its land area to open space. Following a plan called New Ways to the Water, Essen is building a 150-kilometer long greenway network to link greenspace along the Ruhr River with the Zollverein Coal Mine UNESCO World Heritage Site and the Emscher Landscape Park, Europe's most comprehensive river-renaturation project. The ongoing conversion of Essen has been so impressive that the European Commission named Essen as the 2017 European Green Capital.

The European Green Capital judges were particularly impressed with Essen's accomplishments in climate action, air quality, noise abatement and water quality. Between 1990 and 2011, Essen reduced its CO_2 emissions by almost 30 percent even though 140,000 commuters enter the City every day. Essen also targets CO_2 emission reductions of 40 percent by 2020 and 95 percent by 2050 compared with 1990, which is substantially more ambitious than the goals established by the European Union, Germany and the State of North Rhine-Westphalia. To reach these targets, Essen formed an independent Climate Agency which helps building owners analyze, plan, finance and complete energy retrofits (Essen, 2014; O'Toole, McEvoy and Campion, 2015).

To control traffic-generated emissions, Essen has expanded its bicycle infrastructure and pledged $234 million euros over a five-year period to improvements in its public transportation system. The City leads by example, employing 100 percent green electricity in its operations and requiring all of its new buildings to meet passive house standards. The 17 buildings in Essen's Gruga Park are served by a local heating district fueled entirely by the park's garden wastes (Essen, 2014; O'Toole, McEvoy and Campion, 2015).

Figure 9-1: *Grupapark is part of a 150-kilometer green-route network.*

To improve the acoustic environment, Essen plans for over half of the population to be within 300 meters of either a quiet area or an even more tranquil natural-countryside quiet area. Improved railway operational procedures, automobile parking routing systems and other transportation-related noise reduction projects have already been undertaken. Perhaps most interesting is Essen's ongoing program of repaving roadway segments with low-noise asphalt (O'Toole, McEvoy and Campion, 2015; EGC, 2015b).

Due to extensive public education, residents here have learned to reduce, reuse and recycle waste to the extent that Essen has not sent any domestic garbage to landfills since the 1960s. The reduced amount of waste still thrown out by households is used to fuel a waste-to-energy plant that generates electricity as well as enough heat to meet 20 percent of the City's total demand through Essen's district heating system (Essen, 2014; O'Toole, McEvoy and Campion, 2015; EGC, 2015b).

Figure 9-2: *The Green Centre of Essen – University District, transformed from a former railroad yard, uses reed/lily islands to filter rainwater within a series of interconnected ponds.*

The Ruhr River supplies Essen's drinking water and the City is in the forefront of water protection strategies. Since 1983, Essen has promoted rainwater collection ponds, raingardens and other forms of decentralized storm water management by offering a reduction in the drainage fees charged for impervious surfaces that empty into public drainage systems. In response, new developments often feature attractive as well as practical water-retention features such as the series of ponds in the University District which use reed and lily-filled islands to filter rainwater. Essen's wastewater treatment plants are also getting attention for developing and testing new technological processes to prevent the contamination of waterways by pharmaceuticals and other micro-pollutants (Essen, 2014; O'Toole, McEvoy and Campion, 2015; EGC, 2015b).

Essen aims to grow by redeveloping infill and brownfield sites. As a prime example, the Green Centre of Essen – University District is being transformed immediately north of downtown on a former railroad freight yard. This project implements Essen's goal of a "city of short distances" by incorporating a mix of residential, commercial and office uses, proximity to major cultural and shopping opportunities, adjacency to the City's central public transportation station and access to the Rhine Rail cycle trail (Essen, 2014).

In other cases, Essen converts brownfields into parkland. For example, lands once occupied by Krupp steel works have been transformed into Krupp Park, which features wooded areas, athletic fields, playgrounds and a lake fed by storm water from the adjacent ThyssenKrupp headquarters (Essen, 2014).

Essen adopted a green area system plan in 1927 that depicted inner and outer greenbelts connected by roughly 17 green corridors plus a dozen green fingers extending toward the City Center. Consistent with this plan, open space was largely retained in the southern greenbelt along the Ruhr River. The closures of coal mines and steelworks that began in the 1960s prompted Essen to create a program in 1975 that created over 100 green areas on former industrial lands and slag heaps in the northern part of the City. Today, green areas and open space account for over half of the City's land area. Furthermore, over 99 percent of Essen residents live within 300 meters of a green area (Essen, 2014; EGC, 2015b).

Since 2007, the City has focused even more on connecting greenspace using a strategy called "Essen – New Ways to the Water", which the European Green Capitals jury praised as an "exemplary initiative" (EGC, 2015a). New Ways to the Water places a 150-kilometer "Green main route network" within 500 meters of more than 250,000 residents. Three north-south corridors within this network link southern green areas along the Ruhr River with restoration projects north of the City including Zollverine Coal Mine UNESCO World Heritage Site and Emscher Landscape Park. As of 2014, over 500 projects had been implemented under New Ways to the Water (Essen, 2014; EGC, 2015b).

Zollverine World Heritage Site occupies 100 hectares of land that once provided the surface operations for a vast underground coal mine. Now a popular tourist destination, Zollverine retains many of its industrial era structures and machines in a landscaped setting and provides a home for athletic competitions, entertainment events, creative industries and cultural facilities, including the Ruhr Museum. The green areas of Zollverein also contribute wildlife habitat, most notably for Peregrine falcons which are reestablishing themselves here after a long absence from North Rhine-Westphalia (Essen, 2014).

Figure 9-3: *Swans and other birds benefit from restoration of the Heisinger Nature Reserve.*

The Emscher River was once the most polluted river in Germany.

Now it is the subject of Europe's most comprehensive river naturalization project. This project, called the Emscher Landscape Park, is a cooperative effort of Essen and five other municipalities aimed at transforming this former wastewater canal and its tributaries into a coherent network of green and blue spaces. By 2020, this consortium will complete the restoration of what were once open sewers into near-natural meandering streams, helping to protect the 109 animal species and 1,500 plant species that live here, including 50 listed species. In addition to promoting biodiversity, Emscher Landscape Park will manage storm water naturally and create a trail system offering recreation, exercise and alternative transportation options for pedestrians and bicyclists (Essen, 2014).

Essen set aside its first nature reserve in 1939. In 2010, Essen pledged to improve wildlife habitat and other ecosystem services by signing the Biodiversity in Municipalities Declaration. Today, conservation protections apply to over 34 percent of the City, including 12 nature reserves and 49 protected landscapes. At 150 hectares, the Heisinger Lowlands is Essen's largest refuge. Heisinger lies on a bend in the Ruhr River and features oxbow lakes, alluvial woodlands and tall oat grass meadows. Despite listing as a Natura 2000 site, parts of Heisinger needed extensive restoration. By removing dumped material, eliminating inconsistent uses and renaturing waterways, the riverbank habitats here have returned to near-natural conditions (Treanor, Connolly and McEvoy, 2014; Essen, 2014). Today Heisinger is a favorite place to take a nature walk and see grey heron, kingfishers, grebe and mute swans (Schulemann-Maier, 2016).

On the bluffs above Heisinger Reserve, Essen has established another nature reserve in the Schellenberger Forest which protects the habitat of pine marten and red fox as well as stands of old-growth oaks. On the many paths in this forest, hikers can also explore the ruins of Schellenberger Castle, originally built in 1240 and destroyed only 48 years later (Schulemann-Maier, 2016).

The 2017 European Green Capital Award recognizes Essen for widespread eco-accomplishments including climate action, noise abatement, waste reduction, brownfield revitalization and the growth of a greenway network connecting largely-restored open space areas constituting over half the land area of the City. Throughout this comprehensive makeover, the City has led by example while also focusing on public education and citizen involvement in its sustainability planning and implementation. Perhaps the European Commission put it best: "The City is making admirable efforts to establish itself as a 'City in transformation' that is overcoming a challenging history to reinvent itself as a 'Green City' and a leading example for others. The City credits its citizens and their ability to change as key to this success and this ethos is visible through their application tag line "ESSENtials – changing the way we act"" (EGC, 2015c).

CHAPTER 10

Nijmegen, Netherlands: Room for the river

Nijmegen, 2018 European Green Capital, fights climate change with renewable energy, compact development and a transportation system that puts bicycles in the driver's seat. However, this city of 171,000 people, 40 miles southeast of Amsterdam, recognizes that climate change adaptation is also needed. To prepare for increasingly severe storms, Nijmegen is converting its downtown to permeable green infrastructure as well as enlarging the Waal River floodplain and creating new civic places, recreational spaces and wildlife habitat in the process.

Over half of all homes in The Netherlands are vulnerable to flooding. A worst-case flood could inundate half the country, affecting 10 million people. The Waal River, which makes a sharp right turn at Nijmegen, jumped its banks in 1993 and 1995, forcing the evacuation of 250,000 people. For centuries, the Dutch responded to flooding by building higher dikes. But the increasingly extreme storms resulting from climate change have prompted a new approach: moving the dikes back to make room for ever-expanding rivers. In the 1990s, The Netherlands studied 100 bottlenecks and picked 39 projects based on many criteria including the enthusiasm of the local citizenry (ClimateWire, 2012; HUD User, 2015).

With a price tag of $460 million, Nijmegen's "Room for the River" is the most expensive of these 39 projects. Aimed at defending against a 1,250-year flood, Nijmegen and its partners have relocated the old dikes, dug a secondary, three-kilometer-long channel and formed a new island which will feature parkland, performance space, bike paths and pedestrian promenades. The design also creates room for nature, improving stream ecology and adding 30 different types of habitat including mudflats, meadows and forests. In conjunction with other projects upstream and downstream, Nijmegen is helping to repopulate the Waal River and its re-contoured floodplain with sturgeon, beaver, sea eagles and otter. Scheduled for completion in 2016, this project has already won international awards for innovatively combining water management with urban redevelopment and environmental restoration (ClimateWire, 2012; HUD User, 2015; Nijmegen, 2015).

Figure 10-1: *The footbridge links downtown Nijmegen with the farms, woods, trails and cycle paths of Ooijpolder.*

Projections of future flash flooding have motivated Nijmegen to replace concrete and other impervious surfaces using landscaping elements that disconnect pavement from water systems and reuse storm water while creating more attractive urban environments. Together with eight partners in five countries, Nijmegen formed a group called Future Cities aimed at adapting to climate change as well as mitigating it. Future Cities urges communities to "enjoy adaptation." In response, Nijmegen prepared a plan called Green Allure Inner City that shows how the city center can be beautified as well as fortified by building pocket parks, gardens and topiary while making streets, roofs and even walls literally green. To put this plan in action, Nijmegen replaced parking lots and vacant parcels with parks, re-landscaped streets and subsidized the installation of 40 green roofs (Frehmann and Althoff, 2010; Future Cities, 2013; Nijmegen, 2007; Nijmegen, 2015).

The Nijmegen plan envisions a compact city surrounded by a green belt that is easily accessible on foot or by bicycle. The Ooijpolder forms the eastern segment of this greenbelt, offering miles of walking and bicycling opportunities only a footbridge away from downtown. In addition to agricultural land and historic sites, natural areas make Ooijpolder one of ten ecological hotspots in Nijmegen's greenbelt. Over 600 hectares of the southeastern portion of the greenbelt were formerly used as a military training area but are now protected as natural forests and heathlands. Until recently, the Waal River formed Nijmegen's northern border and the river's floodplain served as the northern segment of the greenbelt. However, Nijmegen and its partners are now building an eco-friendly community north of the Waal River as well as Park Lingezegen, a 1,700-hectare greenspace with distinct subareas for recreation, agriculture, nature and conservation of water resources. Lengezegen Park also creates a buffer with the City of Arnhem and effectively serves as the new northern segment of the greenbelt (Nijmegen, 2015; Park Lingezegen, 2016).

In addition to retaining its greenbelt, Nijmegen holds the line against sprawl by carefully redeveloping vacant or underused properties. Limospark is a former military barracks that Nijmegen and its partners transformed into a 15-hectare mixed-use development featuring a school, restaurant and art studio as well as apartments within a parklike setting. In downtown Nijmegen, the Hessenberg project transformed a former newspaper/printing complex into a ten-building mini-neighborhood of apartments and

Figure 10-2: *Nijmegen retained the original pedestrian walkways in Hessenberg.*

retail space within an intricate network of gardens, courtyards and pedestrian alleyways reflecting this district's pre-automobile history. In contrast with the current demand for "starchitecture", Hessenberg emphasizes quality public space over flamboyant building design (Europaconcorsi. 2015; Nijmegen, 2015).

Nijmegen aims to be energy neutral by 2045 with the help of 16 wind turbines, a million solar panels, 40,000 solar boilers, 11,000 households on district heating systems plus increased reliance on biomass and geothermal. Nijmegen is already off to a good start, reducing per capita CO_2 emissions by over 16 percent between 2008 and 2014. Much of this success resulted from commitments to reduce fossil fuel dependency in Nijmegen's largest companies and institutions including the city and public utilities. After two rounds of energy covenants, these organizations had saved almost 300,000 tons of CO_2, a 36 percent reduction. In 2016, Nijmegen will begin converting GDF Suez, a huge coal fired power plant, to an assortment of renewable sources including solar, biomass and wind (European Commission, 2016; Nijmegen, 2015).

Figure 10-3: *Bicycles account for 64 percent of Nijmegen's commuter traffic.*

Nijmegen's transportation system also deserves credit for mitigating climate change. Streets are clearly categorized as "access" (with adjacent bike lanes physically separated from motor traffic) or "traffic limited" (where speeds are limited to 30 kilometers per hour). Nijmegen built three bike bridges over the Waal River plus parking spaces for 5,200 bikes in downtown and 8,700 bikes in at the railway station. Nijmegen also offers 43 kilometers of bicycle superhighways and plans to expand its network to 80 kilometers. These bicycle superhighways extend to nearby cities as well as major destinations within Nijmegen including a university with 19,000 students. On the 16-kilometer bike superhighway called the RijnWaalpad, bicyclists have priority at most intersections, allowing a 45-minute spin between the City of Arnhem and Nijmegen, within a corridor that is home to 12,000 work sites (Bicycle Dutch, 2015; Bicycle Dutch 2016a; European Commission, 2016; Nijmegen, 2015).

Nijmegen has made the city easy to navigate by bicycle and the people have responded by bicycling. This city of 171,000 residents is home to 250,000 bicycles. Bicycles account for 64 percent of all commuter traffic here and represent 37 percent of all trips of 7.5 kilometers or less, a larger percent than cars. In 2016, the Netherlands Cycling Union picked Nijmegen as The Cycling City of The Netherlands (Bicycle Dutch, 2016b; European Commission, 2016; Nijmegen, 2015). This recognition, plus its accomplishments in green structure, infill development and climate change mitigation/adaptation, explain why the European Commission selected Nijmegen as the 2018 European Green Capital.

CHAPTER 11

Freiburg, Germany: Doing well by doing good

F reiburg deserves its "Green City" brand. This 220,000-person city on the edge of the Black Forest in southeastern Germany has consistently been in the forefront of all things sustainable, from renewable energy and eco-neighborhoods to alternative transportation and preservation of the natural environment. By building a robust economy with the help of green institutes, firms and jobs, Freiburg also exemplifies the motto of "doing well by doing good".

In 1975, protests at the construction site of a nuclear power plant near Freiburg are often credited with giving birth to the green movement. Following the 1986 Chernobyl nuclear disaster, Freiburg dedicated itself to a solar future. In 1992, Freiburg was named Germany's Environmental Capital. Freiburg has consistently won similar recognition ever since, including the European Public Transport Award, the German Solar Award and the Federal Awards for Sustainability in Urban Development (Freiburg, 2008).

Freiburg is probably best known as a world leader in saving energy, renewable energy and development of energy-efficient technologies. In 2007, Freiburg retrofitted all 2,026 residences in the Weingarten-West neighborhood and retooled a 40-year old, 16-story residential tower to meet passive solar standards, reducing heating demand by 80 percent. This was Germany's first Passive House high-rise (Freiburg, 2011).

Freiburg is growing its reliance on renewable energy including hydropower, biomass, biogas and solar. As a unique illustration, Freiburg has seven small hydroelectric plants partly fed by the "Bachle", tiny water canals restored to streets in the pedestrian zone of the historic city center. Leading by example, Freiburg trams are powered entirely by renewable energy from hydroelectric, wind and solar sources (Freiburg, 2011).

Figure 11-1: *Tiny water canals, or Bachle, restore historic character to Freiburg's downtown pedestrian zone.*

As of 2009, over 1,000 photovoltaic collectors covered the rooftops of Freiburg's public and private buildings, annually generating 15 megawatts, enough to power 5,500 two-person households for one year. Perhaps the most famous symbols of "Solar City" Freiburg are the photovoltaic array atop the soccer stadium and Heliotrope, the completely solar-powered 1994 house that rotates for maximum sunlight capture. Not content with these accomplishments,

Freiburg aims to put solar collectors on every home in the City. In fact, if solar panels are not installed on a new dwelling, the City requires that the roof at least be built to accommodate solar photovoltaic or thermal systems in the future (Freiburg, 2011).

The solar industry is also key to Freiburg's economic development strategy. Since 1981, Freiburg has been home to Europe's largest institute for applied solar energy research, with 800 employees consulting worldwide. This institute as well as other sustainability organizations support Freiburg's claim as the foremost center for solar energy knowledge transfer. In response to this green industry strategy, the Freiburg region now has 2,000 solar enterprises generating 650 million euro per year and employing 12,000 workers. As an additional economic boost, an estimated 25,000 "specialist tourists" visit Freiburg each year to learn about its solar and other sustainability successes (Freiburg, 2011). These successes add luster to Freiburg's Solar City and Green City brands and create a positive feedback loop, attracting potential innovators from around the world who often decide to move here, consequently strengthening green industries and building support for sustainable public policies (Rohracher and Spath, 2012).

Freiburg is committed to technologies that increase energy efficiency, particularly cogeneration plants that produce electricity as well as heat. A total of 140 cogeneration plants produced roughly half of the City's energy needs as of 2009. The cogeneration plant in Rieselfeld uses natural gas for district heating and electricity. The Vauban ecodistrict takes the extra step of powering its cogeneration plant with wood chips (Freiburg, 2011).

Freiburg's Land Use Plan fights sprawl by promoting "inner development". Since 1980, over half of Freiburg's residential construction has been on infill sites, particularly underutilized industrial areas and former military bases. The Land Use Plan 2020, adopted in 2006, reduced the land designated for development by 30 hectares (Freiburg, 2008). A sophisticated land use analysis estimates that up to 95 percent of the development demand projected to the year 2030 can be accommodated within the City's current boundaries (Freiburg, 2011).

Figure 11-2: *Frequent tram service makes car ownership unnecessary in Freiburg's Vauban neighborhood.*

Freiburg's most famous example of inner development is the transformation of the Vauban district from military uses to a compact neighborhood of predominantly four-story buildings. Residents with cars can drive on the traffic-calmed streets of Vauban for passenger pick-up/drop-off and deliveries, but parking is confined to structures at the perimeter of the district. As a result, Vauban is by far Germany's largest car-free project (Berrini and Bono, 2010). Instead of owning cars, residents here are encouraged to walk, bike and use a tram line directly linking Vauban with downtown. In fact, only 82 residents per 1,000 own cars in Vauban as compared with 430 cars per 1,000 residents in Freiburg as a whole and 550 cars per 1,000 in Germany (Medearis and Daseking, 2012).

About 240 residences in Vauban use passive solar and the rest comply with low energy construction standards that consume only 65kWh per square meter per year. A carbon-neutral cogeneration plant supplies heating as well as electrical power to 700 households and ubiquitous rooftop photovoltaic solar collectors create enough electricity to power 200 dwelling units (Freiburg, 2011). Perhaps most important, Vauban is a pleasant place to live, with gardens and landscaped courtyards plus tree-lined streets where people can easily walk or bike to schools, shopping, entertainment venues, community centers and nearby tram stops.

Rieselfeld is another model ecodistrict. Used for surface wastewater spreading until the 1980s, this 70-hectare site has become home to over 10,000 residents in buildings with optimal solar orientation served by a district heating system. As in the Vauban, Rieselfeld is linked to downtown Freiburg by a direct tram line and the Freiburg bicycle network. A soil filter treats all rainwater before it flows into the western half of Rieselfeld, which has become a 205-hectare nature reserve and European bird sanctuary, providing habitat for white storks, stonechats and red-backed shrike (Freiburg, 2008; Freiburg, 2011).

In the 1960s, Freiburg adopted an integrated transportation planning approach that includes pedestrians, bicyclists and public transit. More than 80 percent of Freiburg residents live within 500 meters of a tram stop. Remarkably, Freiburg trams and busses carry 200,000 passengers per day within a region of 250,000 people (Freiburg, 2011).

In 1973, Freiburg transformed much of its downtown to a pedestrian zone where private vehicles are limited to deliveries and local residents. In the 1990s, Freiburg changed the speed limit on non-arterial streets to 30 kilometers per hour which greatly improved safety while reducing traffic noise and pollution. Today, 90 percent of Freiburg's residents live in neighborhoods with 30 kph speed limits. Freiburg's 420-km bike network incorporates 170 km of bike paths, 120 km of forest/service roads and 130 km of bike-friendly streets with 30 kph speed limits. (Freiburg, 2011). As a result, 30 percent of all Freiburg trips are done by bicycle and another 15 percent occur on foot (Medearis and Daseking, 2012).

Freiburg owns almost one third of the land within its borders and of this amount, more than half is protected from development by some form of nature designation (Medearis and Daseking, 2012). At 5,139 hectares, Freiburg owns Germany's largest communal forest. The eastern portion of the city forest features the coniferous trees of the Black Forest while the lowland portions to the west are called Mooswald or moss forests composed of deciduous riparian woodlands. Roughly 90 percent of the forest is in natural conservation and almost half is designated as Natura 2000. Immediately abutting downtown, residents and tourists can easily spend a few hours or a few days exploring the forest's 450-km trail network (Freiburg, 2011).

From a Freiburg bus stop, skiers, bicyclists and hikers can transfer to a gondola for a ride to the top of Schauinsland Mountain, one of the highest peaks in the Black Forest. Schauinsland is famous for the wind-twisted trees found in these high-altitude pasturelands which now serve as a cultural landscape. Freiburg uses environment-friendly management practices here to protect habitat for lynx, chamois, three-toed woodpeckers and over 120 endangered plant and animal species (Freiburg, 2011).

Figure 11-3: *Vineyards on the Schlossberg green corridor literally overlook central Freiburg.*

Tuniberg is Freiburg's own vineyard district, capitalizing on a Mediterranean climate and rocky terrain to produce a Burgundy-style wine since the Roman era. With assistance from the Freiburg Environmental Protection Office, vintners here have been switching from industrial farming habits to nature friendly techniques including the elimination of hazardous pesticides. As a result, endangered lizards, birds and insects are making a comeback here (Freiburg, 2011).

After World War II, Freiburg began to spread west, consuming roughly 100 hectares of its lowland forest, or Mooswald. In 1997, Freiburg prevented further encroachment, creating a 44 square-kilometer landscape conservation area that is now part of the European Natura 2000 system. Today, Mooswald offers protection to rare species of beetles, bats and woodpeckers as well recreation for birders and nature lovers (Freiburg, 2011).

Although perhaps not as explicit as in some European cities, Freiburg's open spaces form a green structure. Roughly 500 hectares of green areas link the heart of the City with a surrounding green belt (Freiburg, 2008). On a pedestrian bridge from the downtown pedestrian zone, walkers can easily access a labyrinth of trails in Schlossberg, the green corridor east of the City. The green belt encircling Freiburg incorporates portions of the Black Forest, Schauinsland Mountain, Mooswald, the Rieselfeld nature reserve and the vineyards of Tuniberg as well as smaller green spaces like Seepark, created for a 1986 garden expo, and Mundenhof, Freiburg's wildlife and nature park.

Freiburg understands that public involvement is important to achieving its sustainability goals. Well-informed citizens and experts routinely conduct lively debates at community meetings and events (Rohracher and Spath, 2012). Roughly one quarter of Freiburg residents participate in organizations dedicated to planning, environmental protection and community improvements. For example, 50 schools, churches and other groups have become stream sponsors, which often involves the removal of invasive species and the restoration of native aquatic habitat (Freiburg, 2011). Though engagement, Freiburg encourages citizens to take pride in the City's alternative transportation, renewable energy and species preservation accomplishments while motivating them to build an even greener green city.

CHAPTER 12

Torres Vedras, Portugal: Rediscovering wind power

Torres Vedras excels at renewable energy generation and ecotourism, featuring extensive trail systems and a walkable, compact city center. The municipality also conducts an extensive citizen education program emphasizing the lifestyle choices needed to achieve sustainability and the public support helpful to attracting green businesses. Consequently, Torres Vedras was one of the first two cities to win the European Green Leaf Award. Similar to the European Green Capitals Award, which is geared toward cities with a population of more than 100,000, the European Commission grants its Green Leaf prize to cities of between 20,000 and 100,000 population based on a competitive process judged by a panel of experts. In the case of the 2015 European Green Leaf Award, Torres Vedras, a coastal city of 80,000 people 25 miles north of Lisbon, was one of two winners out of an original field of eight applicants.

The ridgelines of Torres Vedras are studded with small, historic windmills, a few of which are still in use. Torres Vedras has super-sized this ancient technology with nine wind farms currently generating 112 MWh. In its effort to be a leader in renewable energy, Torres Vedras plans to expand wind turbine capacity to 332 GWh, which would supply the city's entire electrical energy demand (Torres Vedras, 2014).

Figure 12-1: *Modern wind turbines share hilltops with historic windmills in Torres Vedras.*

The Torres Vedras Mobility Strategy led to the creation of the Agostinhas bike share system, which offers 290 bikes at 14 stations. Over 50km of bike paths are available, including one providing a safe route for children to bike to school. The strategy also calls for extending the pedestrian network within the historic city center, an area that is already remarkably walkable due to the inherent traffic calming effect of old, narrow streets as well as outright car prohibitions on several lanes, particularly those near the medieval castle (Portugal, 2015).

Figure 12-2: *Pedestrian lanes and narrow streets calm and often eliminate motorized traffic in Torres Vedras.*

Torres Vedras has created 255 km of trails, offering a wide range of hiking experiences. History buffs looking for exercise can walk between and within the Lines of Torres Vedras, the name given to the network of 152 forts completed by the British and Portuguese in 1810 to keep Napoleon's army out of Lisbon. Hikers on the Torres Vedras Eco-Trail pass farms and vineyards on their way up to the summit of the Socorro and Archeira Mountains, which the city has saved as a Protected Landscape and where it has built an Interpretive

Center that facilitates hiking, birding and a deeper understanding of the local ecology. Torres Vedras is also home to a segment of the Atlantic Path, the European trail that parallels the entire shoreline from St. Petersburg, Russia to Tarifa, Spain. Walkers on this portion of the Atlantic Path are treated to Natura 2000 wetlands, birding opportunities, historic landmarks, cultural sites, rocky cliffs, pristine beaches and a lively resort scene in the coastal town of Santa Cruz (Torres Vedras, 2014).

Figure 12-3: *The Atlantic Path passes Guincho Rock on the Torres Vedras coastline.*

Sustainability requires personal lifestyle choices as well as governmental policies and technological fixes. We have to actually adopt and routinely practice planet-friendly behaviors in order to live within the earth's carrying capacity (Moore, 2015). As noted by the European Green Leaf judges, Torres Vedras is heavily committed to public involvement (European Commission, 2014). In 2013, the city opened its Centre for Environmental Education, which incorporates state-of the-art technology including the conversion of solar, wind and geothermal energy into hydrogen fuel (Portugal, 2015). In addition to showcasing innovations, the Centre conducts programs and training sessions on energy efficiency, alternative energy, carbon-free mobility, waste reduction/recycling and water quality/conservation for a projected 8,000 annual participants (Torres Vedras, 2014). Torres Vedras considers an informed and engaged citizenry as essential to achieving its vision of a thriving, sustainable community with a high quality of life powered by green industries and eco-tourism.

CHAPTER 13

Oslo, Norway: The blue and the green and the city in between

On Oslo's green subway line, passengers board a train in the city center and step off at Sognsvann Lake to hike, bike, fish, swim or simply contemplate nature. Backpackers use the Sognsvann transit station as a gateway to the network of trails that thread through the Marka, the 301-square kilometer forested greenbelt that forms two-thirds of Oslo's total land area. Oslo is also securing and restoring the Akerselva River corridor as it plunges through the heart of the city on its way from the Marka to the Oslo fiord. Through a succession of plans beginning with the 1917-18 parks plan, the city has committed itself to ultimately daylighting and restoring all eight of the rivers that once flowed freely to the sea. To accommodate significant growth pressure while protecting the Marka and expanding greenways, Oslo is implementing compact development citywide and creating highly successful waterfront revitalization projects. These efforts have prompted a leading expert to recognize Oslo as a good example of a biophilic city (Beatley, 2012).

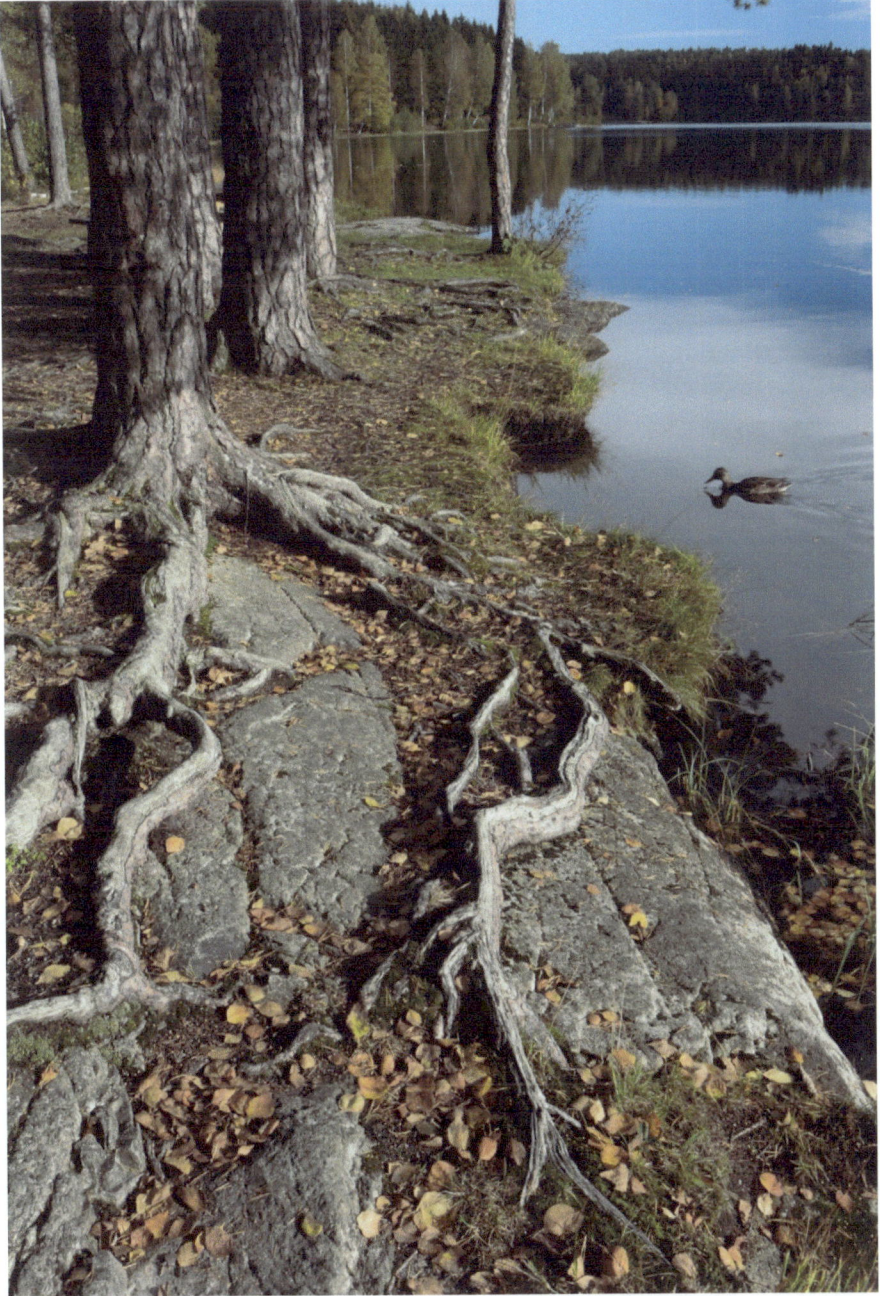

Figure 13-1: *Sognsvann Lake in the Marka, the forested greenbelt that forms two thirds of Oslo's total land area .*

Biophilic cities protect the environment and link residents with nature, an essential ingredient of human productivity, health and happiness. Oslo's motto, "the blue and the green and the city in between", establishes the proximity of the Marka and the Oslo fiord while suggesting that the blue and the green are just as important as the urbanized portions of the city.

Statistics from Oslo's application to the European Green Capital competition support the city's biophilic credentials. Over 94 percent of Oslo residents live within 300 meters of greenspace. The Marka alone is home to 70 lakes for swimming, 100 rivers and lakes for fishing and 460 km of bicycle trails. Even within the developed portions of the city, roughly 19 percent of the land area is publicly-accessible greenspace (Oslo, 2008).

Figure 13-2: *Oslo has converted the banks of the Akerselva River from an abandoned industrial zone into a major arts and recreation corridor.*

Oslo's blue-green evolution did not occur overnight. The city's first parks plan, adopted in 1917-18, envisioned radial greenways, or green fingers, following the river corridors connecting the Marka and the fiord. Subsequent plans built on that concept, calling for higher density development within centers connected by trails linking schools, sporting fields and other community facilities as well as open space and the surrounding Marka. Throughout the 20th Century, implementation of this vision was slowed by world events and local economic conditions. But over time, Oslo succeeded in largely transforming the banks of the Akerselva River from a declining industrial district to Akerselva Environmental Park, which showcases the river with greenspace, trails, new development and historic factory buildings repurposed as restaurants, studios, entertainment venues, offices and housing (Jorgensen and Kine, 2012).

Oslo has low carbon emissions per capita because this city generates almost all of its power hydroelectrically and uses that renewable energy to fuel its highly-developed metro rail public transportation system. In 2005, Oslo adopted a climate and energy action plan aimed at reducing greenhouse gas emissions 50 percent by 2030 as compared to 1990 levels. The ten-point plan for reaching that goal included a requirement that all new municipal buildings comply with passive/low energy standards and that that fossil fuel heating be completely eliminated in all municipal buildings by 2020. The plan also calls for enlargement of Oslo's district heating network in conjunction with an expansion of the waste-to-energy plant and installation of a new bioenergy plant (European Commission, 2009; Oslo 2008).

Despite having the fastest growth rate of all European capitals, Oslo has maintained its enviable relationship with nature by promoting compact, infill development. Between 2002 and 2006, 80 percent of all new development occurred on previously developed land and brownfield sites (Oslo, 2008). Special attention has been focused on three waterfront areas no longer needed for shipbuilding and other port activities, collectively known as Fiord City. These areas are connected by Harbor Promenade, a nine-kilometer interpretive trail that invites pedestrians and cyclists to learn the history of the waterfront, including the Akershus Fortress, the medieval castle overlooking Fiord City.

Located toward the western end of the Harbor Promenade, the Aker Brygge district now occupies the site of a ship building firm that closed in 1982. This redevelopment project, built in the 1980s and 1990s, was recognized by urban guru Jan Gehl for its judicious mix of office, residential, retail and entertainment uses. Gehl adds that although the density is high, "…it's the right kind of density…" thanks to careful design of the buildings and public spaces, which give pedestrians endless opportunities for walking, relaxing and dining at the water's edge (Gehl, 2010).

Tjuvholmen, the second phase of Fiord City, was once a prison island. Today it is home to several high-rise buildings including the luxurious Thief Hotel. People are motivated to cross the pedestrian bridge from Aker Brygge to Tjuvholmen by the sight of the curvilinear Astrup Fearnley Museum of Modern Art designed by Renzo Piano.

Figure 13-3: *The Astrup Fearnley Art Museum on Tjuvholmen, which literally means thief island.*

Bjorvika, the third phase of Fiord City, will ultimately locate 20,000 work sites and 5,000 residences between the central train station and the waterfront. Parks and other public spaces will eventually cover 40 percent of Bjorvika. The marble-clad Opera House, which serves as the focal point for this district, features a sloping roof that people can climb for a 360-degree panorama of, quite-fittingly, the blue, the green and the city in between.

CHAPTER 14

Munster, Germany: City of short distances

I n 2004, LivCom named Munster as the most livable city on earth in its size category. This city of 300,000 people, 250 miles west of Berlin, was also named as the Climate Protection Capital of Germany in 2010 and Germany's Bicycle Capital in 2014. In 2010-2011, Munster was a finalist for European Green Capital. Although Stockholm and Hamburg won that competition, the European Green Capital judges were particularly impressed with Munster's commitment to ecomobility and its evolving network of interconnected greenbelts and green wedges.

Munster adopted a green structure policy in 1965 that continues to guide development as well as the promotion of greenspace, recreation and biodiversity. The green structure consists of three green belts and seven green wedges that place roughly 95 percent of the population within 300 meters of greenspace. Munster created its inner green belt, the Promenade, on the site of the former fortifications originally surrounding the historic city center. The Promenade's formal landscaping design features lime trees that shade a walking path and separate cycle track, encouraging ecomobility as detailed below (Munster, 2009).

Munster's most prominent green wedge follows the Aa River. Narrow paths and footbridges allow pedestrians to traverse the entire city center with the Aa River often by their side. Once outside the downtown, the City has built its most prominent park on the river banks and attracts visitors with boathouses, museums and a zoo as well as a landscaping design that retains woodlands and wetlands. The other green wedges include a restored 19th Century park, the corridor of a renatured stream and the transformation of a former military range into Peace Park. Munster is not content to rest on its sustainability accomplishments. Between 1998 and 2008, the City grew its green areas by ten percent (Munster, 2009).

Figure 14-1: *Several streets in the center of Munster are reserved for pedestrians, bikes and buses.*

The green structure also connects greenspace within the City of Munster to the Munsterland park landscape, a 6,000-square kilometer cultural landscape characterized by churches, monasteries and moated castles dotting a countryside of hedges, meadows, fields and woods. Despite being actively farmed, the Munsterland park landscape creates habitat for a large diversity of species as well as recreation for locals and tourists (Munster, 2016a). From the heart of Munster, cyclists can follow a 960-kilometer route through Munsterland linking over 100 historic manors, country estates and castles (Munster, 2016a).

Figure 14-2: *The Promenade, a tree-shaded bike-pedestrian path, completely encircles Munster's historic center.*

Munster has fully embraced "ecomobilty" as its transportation goal as well as the shorthand description of its emphasis on walking, public transit and particularly bicycling. Munster has made it safer to pedal by adopting a 30 kilometer per hour (19 mph) speed limit on all residential streets. The City has 450 kilometers of cycle paths in addition to 255 kilometers of cycle paths off of main roads (Munster, 2016b). Many of these cycle paths radiate from the Promenade, the 4.5-kilometer multi-use path completely encircling the city center.

The Promenade is also located less than 1,000 feet from the Munster train station and the Radstation, Germany's largest bicycle garage, offering bicycle repair, sales and lockers as well as 3,300 bike boxes. From the Promenade, cyclists arriving by train or directly from home can navigate to downtown streets that are reserved for buses, pedestrians and, of course, bicyclists. Not surprisingly, 37.6 percent of all trips in Munster are by bicycle, with another 15.6 percent occurring on foot and 10.4 by public transportation. At a mode split of 36.4 for motor vehicles, more people in Munster travel by bicycle than by car (Munster, 2009).

Figure 14-3: *The Munster Radstation, with 3,300 bike boxes, is the largest bicycle garage in Germany*

"City of short distances" is Munster's land use mantra. To achieve its goal of "inner development before outer development" Munster has built one-third of its new housing on infill sites and initiated the conversion of 250 hectares of former port and military facilities. For example, between 2005 and 2007, 62 percent of all new multi-family residential units were built in these redevelopment opportunity areas (Munster, 2009).

Some of these developments have been recognized as models of sustainability, such as Car-Free Garden City Weissenburg, a residential complex on the site of former military grounds. Weissenburg features substantial open space, green roofs, total rainwater recycling and energy-saving building design (Munster, 2016c). In addition, the development is car free. Weissenburg residents cannot own cars but instead rely on buses, bicycling and a car sharing station located at the edge of the development. Weissenburg abuts a cycle track linked to Munster's extensive bicycle network; consequently, over half of its residents bike to work and 67 percent shop by bicycle (Baumer, 2009).

Green structure, ecomobility and infill development accomplishments together helped Munster reduce carbon dioxide emissions by more than 20 percent between 1990 and 2005 and position the city to reach its target of achieving a 40 percent reduction by 2020 (Munster, 2009). In 2015, Munster won another battle against climate change, becoming the first German city to divest its pension fund of oil, gas and all other fossil fuels, explaining that such investments are incompatible with the City's climate protection goals (Mattauch, 2015).

CHAPTER 15

Mollet del Valles, Spain: Agriculture as recreation

Mollet del Valles has beautifully merged conservation, local sustainable agriculture, historic preservation, environmental education and recreational open space in Gallecs, a greenbelt that occupies half of the land area of this city of 52,000 people. The trails here are heavily used by bicyclists, birders and hikers as well as gardeners on their way to tend numerous individual plots tucked within fields, forests and riparian corridors. Gallecs offers a world-class lesson in building support for preservation by ensuring that the public as a whole can personally experience the sights, sounds and smells of a primarily agricultural landscape.

In the 1970s, Gallecs seemed destined to be converted to housing developments serving Barcelona, only ten miles to the south. However, the people of Mollet del Valles and surrounding communities refused to accept suburban sprawl as an inevitability. After decades of uncertainty, preservation was finally assured in 2009 when the government of Catalonia added almost 700 hectares of Gallecs to its PEIN (Plan for Areas of Natural Interest) (Consorci de Gallecs, 2015). PEIN is a network of 165 Catalonian sites protected for their ecological significance (Mollet del Valles, 2014; MEET,

2014).

In addition to preserving Gallecs, Mollet del Valles and its partners launched several environmental revitalization projects. Riverbanks were strengthened and wetlands were created to control, capture and treat storm water as well as improve habitat for waterfowl and other wildlife. Indigenous vegetation was planted to restore several degraded areas including a former motor cross circuit. Gallecs also affiliated with the largest network of nature conservation organizations in Europe (European Commission, 2015a).

Figure 15-1: *The Gallecs greenbelt occupies half of Mollet del Valles.*

The Gallecs plan emphasizes agriculture as the main component of economic and social sustainability balanced by environmental protection and compatible public uses including recreation. The Gallegos Consortium was formed to help implement these goals, beginning with an emphasis on organic farming as a nature-friendly way to produce healthy, locally-grown foods and nurture young farmers (Consorci de Gallecs, 2015). Many of these organic foods are served in the cafeterias of 11 schools, three kindergartens and two facilities for the disabled in Mollet del Valles (URBACT, 2015).

The Consortium collaborates with the Gallegos Agroecological Association and Slow Food Gallegos to promote sustainable rural development through ecological farming practices plus the restoration of ancient wheat varieties and other traditional Gallecs crops. The emphasis on food-based self-reliance led to the creation of the "Product Gallecs" brand and establishment of Agrobotiga Gallegos, a store in Gallecs offering over 70 locally-grown products (Consorci de Gallecs, 2015).

Figure 15-2: *Gallecs is home to numerous individually-tended garden plots.*

Organic agriculture has helped restore a diverse ecosystem in Gallecs ranging from butterflies and other insects to reptiles, amphibians, bats, hedgehogs and over sixty bird species. The Gallegos Consortium runs a biodiversity program supported by the regional wildlife recovery center. It also manages 160 hectares in trees to demonstrate conservation and improvement techniques that are good for wildlife as well as sustainable forestry. The Gallegos Consortium estimates that 700,000 people per year take advantage of the environmental educational and recreational opportunities offered in the Gallecs open classroom (Consorci de Gallecs, 2015).

Figure 15-3: *Gallecs' trails and lanes attract bicyclists, hikers and runners.*

In addition to the rejuvenation of farmland and habitat, Mollet del Valles is justifiably proud of the revitalization of several historic landmarks in Gallecs dating back as far as the 10th century. The Church of Santa Maria Gallegos was first consecrated in 1007 and was most recently restored in the 1960s. Today the church is a popular rest stop for trail users and a community focal point immediately adjacent to the Agrobotiga Gallegos (Consorci de Gallecs, 2015).

Mollet del Valles understands that personal behavior is essential to sustainability. For example, the city maintains an environmental information booth at its market and operates sustainability educational projects including the introduction of planet-friendly lifestyles to school children. The city's 50/50 program has been particularly successful, motivating conservation by letting schools and other public facilities keep half of the money resulting from energy savings produced entirely by behavioral changes like turning the lights off when they are not needed (European Commission, 2015b).

The European Commission recognized Mollet del Valles' environmental achievements in 2015 with the European Green Leaf award (shared with Torres Vedras, Portugal). The expert panel for this award found excellence in all categories while singling out achievements in mobility, air quality, noise abatement, waste reduction/recycling and water management (European Commission, 2015). But the Gallecs greenbelt is this city's crowning achievement, demonstrating how the odds of preservation can be greatly improved by making rural areas publicly available for nature appreciation, environmental education and recreation as well as farming.

CHAPTER 16

Helsinki, Finland: Planned for implementation

Helsinki is transforming its docklands and industrial centers into compact multi-use neighborhoods, promoting efficient, energy-saving infrastructure and accommodating a swelling population without sprawling into the countryside. While growing up, this capital city of 600,000 people is also extending a network of green fingers radiating from the Baltic Sea including a corridor encompassing dozens of islands, an open bay, a cove with a Natura 2000 site and a river valley that links with Eco-Viikki, Finland's largest sustainable development.

Helsinki, together with the state government, owns 80 percent of the land within its borders (URBED 2001). Roughly 30 percent of housing production occurs on land leased from the city using plans prepared by the city in accordance with price restrictions and quality standards established by the city (Rinne, 2009). The city uses the annual income of 200 million euros from these ground rents to finance public transportation and other infrastructure improvements (URBED, 2011). This control of the development process greatly facilitates the implementation of Helsinki's plans.

Figure 16-1: *A canal and its adjacent pedestrian paths create a green spine for the former harbor/industrial district of Ruoholahti.*

The Helsinki plan aims to relocate many older port facilities from locations near the city center, creating infill sites for sustainable development (Jaakkola, 2012). The revitalization of the West Harbour area began in the early 1980s in Ruoholahti, a former harbor, warehouse and industrial district roughly one mile west of downtown. To enhance its waterfront image, the city built a canal flanked by greenspace and pedestrian paths that link playgrounds and other amenities here. The Ruoholahti project area is now home to 6,000 residents and 12,000 jobs served by buses, trams and metro rail (Helsinki, 2015).

In addition to port relocation, Helsinki is revitalizing industrial brownfield sites. The neighborhood of Arabianranta surrounds Arabia, at one time Europe's largest ceramics factory. After years of decline, Arabia announced in 2015 that the few remaining jobs at the Helsinki plant would be relocated to other countries (Jokinen, 2015). However, decades ago, Helsinki began planning for this area to transition from a manufacturing district to the Baltic region's preeminent center for art and design. As of 2009, Arabianranta was home to the largest art university in the Nordic countries as well as an art museum/gallery, music conservatory and three art libraries. Artists participated in the planning of Arabianranta and a percent-for-art requirement has produced a district that now draws visitors to its public art trail (Helsinki, 2009). Redevelopment here was also carefully planned to protect the environment. For example, storm-water from the district is captured in rain gardens incorporated within the Arabia waterfront, a component of Helsinki's green-finger network offering recreational opportunities and non-motorized transportation options while safeguarding the adjacent Vantaa River and the nearby Lammasarri Natura 2000 site.

Figure 16-2: *Arabia's art-district ambiance is enhanced by outdoor sculptures like this one, called Desert Wind.*

North of Arabianranta, the 2,791-acre Viikki district protects roughly three quarters of its land area for recreation and nature conservation, including a segment of an evolving greenway extending south to the city center and north to larger urban forests including Sipoonkorpi National Park (Renne, 2009; Helsinki, 2010). In addition to the science campus of the University of Helsinki, this district is home to a neighborhood of homes, schools and day-care centers known as Eco-Viikki, Finland's largest sustainability laboratory (Joss, 2011). Eco-Viikki's structures save energy using building orientation, rooftop solar collectors and photovoltaics. Multi-story apartment buildings here are separated by linear open spaces that provide solar access, rainwater retention, passive recreation and garden plots for nearby residents (Rinne, 2009). Any rainwater not used for gardening is channeled into Viikinoja stream, a former agricultural ditch that has been relocated and reshaped into a meandering brook (Helsinki, 2010). In a 2009 presentation, the Viikki Project Manager stressed that the "… sustainability of a residential area depends first of all on the lifestyle of its inhabitants." (Rinne, 2009). In 2005, some residents reported that Eco-Viikki converted them to a more ecological way of life while others were relieved to find out that, despite the emphasis on waste reduction/recycling, energy/water conservation and gardening, the Eco-Viikki lifestyle was pretty similar to that of other Finnish neighborhoods (Helsinki, 2005; Rinne, 2009).

Public and private green areas cover an estimated 46 percent of Helsinki (Jaakkola, 2012). For over a century, the city has been working toward greater connectivity of its green areas. In 1914, the city adopted a plan to create a green structure in which local parks and other public facilities are linked to linear parks called green fingers that radiate from the waterfront to the farms and forests surrounding the city. Helsinki's 2050 City Plan maintains this tradition by recognizing that densification increases the need for a continuous network of accessible, quality recreational open space (Helsinki, 2013). In addition to linking parks and preserves, Helsinki wants its green fingers to connect recreational centers, schools, shopping districts and workplaces (Jaakkola, 2012). The biggest green finger is Central Park which contains four nature protection areas in its northern segment and connects at its southern end with Cultural Park, home to several public facilities including the Opera House, the botanical garden and the Helsinki Music Center (Helsinki, 2015a). In 2002, the City Planning Department introduced the concept of a highly-ambitious green finger called Helsinki Park, incorporating a river valley, a cove with a Natura 2000 site, the bay adjacent to downtown Helsinki and the archipelago of islands that lie south of the city center in the Baltic Sea, including the historic Suomenlinna Island Fortress, a UNESCO World Heritage Site (Helsinki, 2015b).

Figure 16-3: *Eco-Viikki's green fingers provide solar access as well as garden plots for nearby residents.*

CHAPTER 17

Barcelona, Spain: Olympics as catalyst

Since the dawn of tourism, Barcelona has lured travelers with its vibrant culture and historic urban character. In the past few decades, this coastal city of 1.6 million has also adopted additional ecocity attributes – restoring its relationship with the Mediterranean Sea, preserving its mountain range and pursuing an ambitious green structure plan that uses pedestrian-friendly corridors to link natural areas for the mutual benefit of wildlife and humans.

Barcelona has a well-deserved reputation as a walking city. The narrow streets of the Gothic Quarter continue to favor people rather than cars. Barcelona's most famous street, La Rambla, is a largely-pedestrian boulevard linking Catalonia Square, the city's major public transportation hub, with walkways surrounding the waterfront. Motorized traffic on La Rambla is confined to one, one-way lane on each side of a tiled promenade shaded by stately trees and crammed with cafes, bookstalls and throngs of walkers, bicyclists and people watchers.

Figure 17-1: *Barcelona extended La Rambla by building La Rambla del Mar, a pedestrian bridge into the transformed Barcelona Harbor.*

In preparation for the 1992 Olympics, Barcelona had the good sense to extend this walking experience by undergrounding a highway that had previously separated the end of La Rambla from the waterfront. The City then completed this pedestrian link using La Rambla del Mar, a pedestrian bridge leading to Port Vell, which at that time was a largely abandoned harbor populated by vacant warehouses and idle rail facilities. Finally the city gave people a reason to cross La Rambla del Mar by revitalizing Port Vell with public spaces, a shopping center, movie theater complex, restaurants, bars and the Barcelona aquarium. As a result, almost 75 percent of Barcelona's tourists now visit Port Vell (Iwamiya and Yeh, 2011).

Before 1992, Barcelona largely turned its back to the sea. Using the Olympics as a catalyst, the city created a two-mile-long beach complete with a boardwalk/bike path now lined with bars and restaurants. Overall, preparations for the Olympics expanded the city's inventory of beaches and greenspace by an impressive 78 percent. The price tag for this extreme make-over came to almost $12 billion. But many observers conclude that the investment was well worth the cost, with Barcelona now ranking as the 5th most popular tourist destination in Europe (Taylor, 2012).

Figure 17-2: *The Frank Gehry fish floats above Barcelona's waterfront boardwalk.*

Figure 17-3: *Parc Ciutadella is one of Barcelona's primary biodiversity reservoirs as well as the site of Cascade Fountain.*

Barcelona's pedestrian-friendly reputation is backed by mode-split statistics. Roughly 80 percent of all trips within Barcelona and 56 percent of trips between Barcelona and other cities occur on foot, by bicycle or public transportation. As of 2012, the City's bike share system offered 6,000 bicycles at 420 stations and experienced 40,000 trips per day (Barcelona Yellow, 2016). Regular extensions of bike infrastructure now place 72 percent of the population within 300 meters of Barcelona's bike network (Barcelona, 2013a). Continued emphasis on compact development as well as alternative transportation has produced relatively low annual greenhouse gas emissions of 2.5 tons per person (Barcelona, 2012).

Collserola Natural Park protects much of the coastal mountain range rising above Barcelona. Recognized for its pine, oak and grassland habitats, Collserola Park covers a total area of 8,295 hectares, of which 1,698 hectares are within the Barcelona city limits. Although this one park represents roughly half of the total area of Barcelona's green infrastructure, three urban parks also serve as major biodiversity reservoirs (Barcelona, 2013b): Montjuic, ancient clifftop fortifications that are now home to over 2,000 plant species (Barcelona, 2015); Ciutadella Park, Barcelona's first park; and Three Hills Park, which includes the ever-popular Park Guell, featuring the whimsical architecture of Antoni Gaudi.

With the adoption of the *Green Infrastructure and Biodiversity Plan 2020*, Barcelona has committed itself to the ambitious task of creating green corridors through this densely developed city that connect the three parks mentioned above (plus numerous smaller green spaces) to the four major natural areas surrounding the City: Collserola Nature Park, the Mediterranean coastline, the Besos River corridor in northeastern Barcelona and the Llobregat River corridor in the southwestern corner of the City. These green corridors often use reconfigured public rights-of-way to activate walking, bicycling and public transportation while promoting biodiversity (Barcelona, 2013b). For example, the green corridor linking Ciutadella Park and Collserola Park, improves wildlife continuity while adding widened sidewalks, rest areas, shade trees, a bus lane and a double-segregated bike lane (Barcelona, 2016). This concept nicely illustrates how people and critters alike benefit from the principle of building cities in balance with nature.

CHAPTER 18

Munich, Germany: Compact – urban – green

In 1998, Munich adopted *Perspective Munich*, a new general plan with a promising ecocity mantra: compact – urban - green. To reach that goal, the City has been fighting suburban sprawl by directing growth inward to abandoned rail and airport land as well as downtown infill sites. Munich is also taking steps to protect its vast greenbelt, restore sensitive environmental resources and improve greenway linkages between natural areas and the city center.

Unlike Munster and Hamburg, Munich did not create an inner greenbelt when it dismantled its medieval city walls. In addition, Munich did not preserve most of the historic canal system that could have evolved into a modern greenway network (Oppermann and Pauleit, 2005). Likewise, Munich did not adopt a formal greenspace design at the start of the twentieth century like the green fingers of Copenhagen and Helsinki. Nevertheless, Munich was fortunate to have the Isar River, which has effectively become the backbone of a green structure concept linking the center of Munich with the farms, moors and other open spaces surrounding the city (Pauleit, 2005).

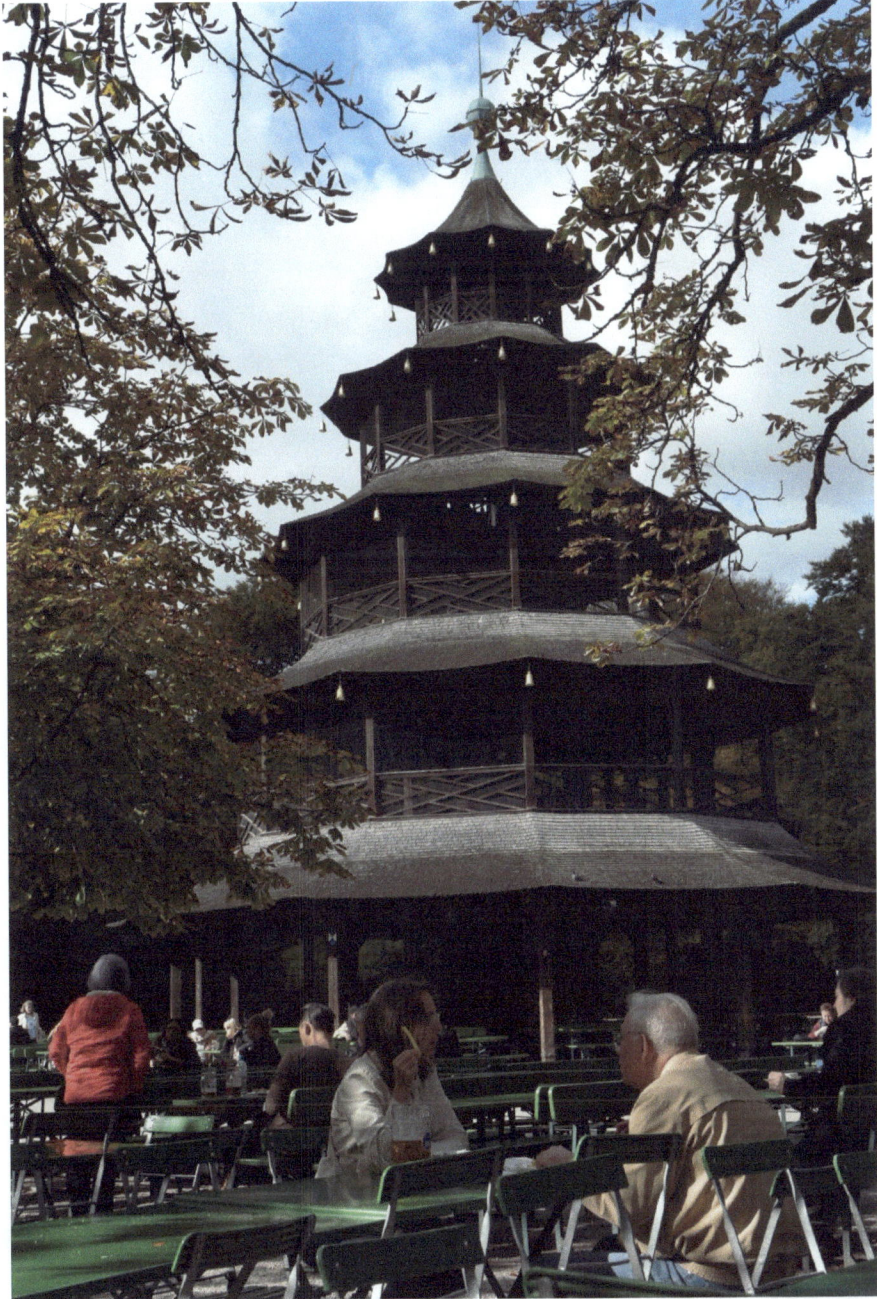

Figure 18-1: *The Chinese Tower beer garden has enhanced the Englisher Garden since 1789.*

The 910-acre Englisher Garden, which parallels the Isar River just north of Munich's historic old town, blends manmade and natural elements. Established in 1789, the park incorporates streams, lakes and woodlands that provide habitat for human-tolerant species. As its name suggests, the Englisher Garden is designed to evoke an idealized, natural landscape. But amongst the greenery are occasional restaurants and two beer gardens. Perhaps most famous is the 7,000-seat beer garden surrounding the Chinese Tower which has burned down and been rebuilt many times, always true to its original 1789 design (Munich, 2016a).

Passing immediately east of the city center, the Isar River and adjacent greenspace give residents a pleasant way to access the Munich greenbelt, a planned and partly-realized network of recreational, agricultural and natural land surrounding and occasionally bisecting the urban area. The 335-square kilometer green belt is primarily used for agriculture, including 3,000 hectares contained in 11 city-owned farms. Six of these farms are cultivated in compliance with organic farming standards, making Munich one of the biggest organic farming concerns in Bavaria (Munich, 2010). The greenbelt's agricultural component also includes 500 herb gardens, small plots of land leased to city dwellers who agree to grow their flowers, fruits and vegetables without the help of chemical fertilizers and pesticides. Commercial farmers in the greenbelt are increasingly adapting to locavore sensibilities by marketing directly to end consumers and partnering with city restaurants and markets (Munich, 2005).

Figure 18-2: *Greenways flanking the Isar River link the city center with the surrounding Munich greenbelt.*

Although many of the regions' natural communities here have been altered by agriculture and urbanization, the public and private sectors are gradually renaturing the moor lands that survived the post-World-War-II growth surge. In 2001, Munich created an eco-account that uses development impact fees to restore key environmental sites like the Eschenreid Moor Lands (Munich, 2005). However, Munich still faces the difficult task of connecting an estimated 153 sites that are currently too small and isolated to fully preserve the city's biodiversity (Pauleit, 2005).

The "green" part of Munich's vision of "compact-urban-green" includes the city's plan to renature the Isar River, the spine of Munich's green structure. The Isar was originally a braided alpine river prone to large, sudden flooding. Beginning in 1889, the Isar was tamed by concrete channels, hydroelectric dams and an upstream reservoir that degraded water quality as well as quantity. By the 1980s, many referred to the Isar as a "dead river". The 1995 Isar Plan aims to resurrect the river by improving its floodwater retention capacity, retooling the riverbanks for recreational greenspace, achieving bathing-level water quality and restoring natural floodplain dynamics needed for wildlife habitat. The Isar cannot entirely return to its natural state since the City basically formed around the manmade engineering of the past century (Oppermann, 2005). Nevertheless, as of 2010, Munich had succeeded in vastly improving eight kilometers of the Isar, creating spawning beds for salmon and other fish as well as beaches, pools and islands that serve as a recreational refuge for the residents of the compact city center (Munich, 2010).

Munich wants to become the cycling capital of Europe. It faces stiff competition from many cities including some profiled in this book. However, the progress to date is impressive. The city boasts two bike-sharing services, 22,000 bike stands and a 1,200-km network of bicycle paths and lanes that is systematically expanding (Munich, 2010; Munich, 2016b).

Several observers rank Munich as among the world's most walkable cities. In the historic center, pedestrian streets radiate from Marienplatz, the large square in front of Munich's neo-Gothic town hall, through retail districts and the farmers market, with connections to the Englisher Garden with its own 78-km network of walking, bicycle and bridle paths and the pedestrian/cycle ways along the Isar that extend into Munich's outlying greenbelt.

Figure 18-3: *Marienplatz lies at the center of Munich's pedestrian network.*

In 1992, Munich opened a new airport, allowing the old airport to become Messestadt Riem, a new town that protects half of its 560-hectare area in open space while using the other half to concentrate an expected 14,000 people and 20,000 jobs. Riem is served by the Munich subway system and follows a mixed-use design that puts employment, housing, retail and open space in close proximity. Riem's greenways extend into residential neighborhoods and a dense network of pedestrian/bicycle trails allows non-motorized access ways to all parts of the new town as well as the countryside. Not coincidentally, Riem is considered a model project, exemplifying the general plan goal to make Munich compact, urban, and green (Munich, 2004).

CHAPTER 19

Salzburg, Austria: Walkability never gets old

Salzburg has earned worldwide recognition largely by keeping its Baroque historic center remarkably intact since the time of Wolfgang Amadeus Mozart, its most famous son. But the city's natural setting is equally impressive due to preservation of the surrounding hills, the Salzach River and Mirabell Gardens, which together form a blue-green network around and through the Old Town, or Altstadt. Salzburg strictly limits car access in this area and encourages alternative transportation using a pathway system that makes walking and bicycling pleasurable as well as the most efficient modes of travel.

In 1996, UNESCO inscribed the historic Salzburg center as a World Heritage Site for its wealth of architectural gems, including Gothic buildings dating from the late-Middle Ages. But the UNESCO honor is also based in part on the integrity of the townscape and urban fabric (UNESCO, 2015a). This feeling of authenticity is arguably enhanced by the fact that Salzburg prohibits non-essential motor vehicles on more than five miles of pavement within the boundaries of the 236-hectare World Heritage Site, which incorporates Monchsberg Mountain, Kapuzinerberg Mountain, Mirabell Gardens and the Salzach River as well as Altstadt (UNESCO, 2015b).

Figure 19-1: *Salzburg has protected Monchsberg Mountain and many of its ancient fortifications.*

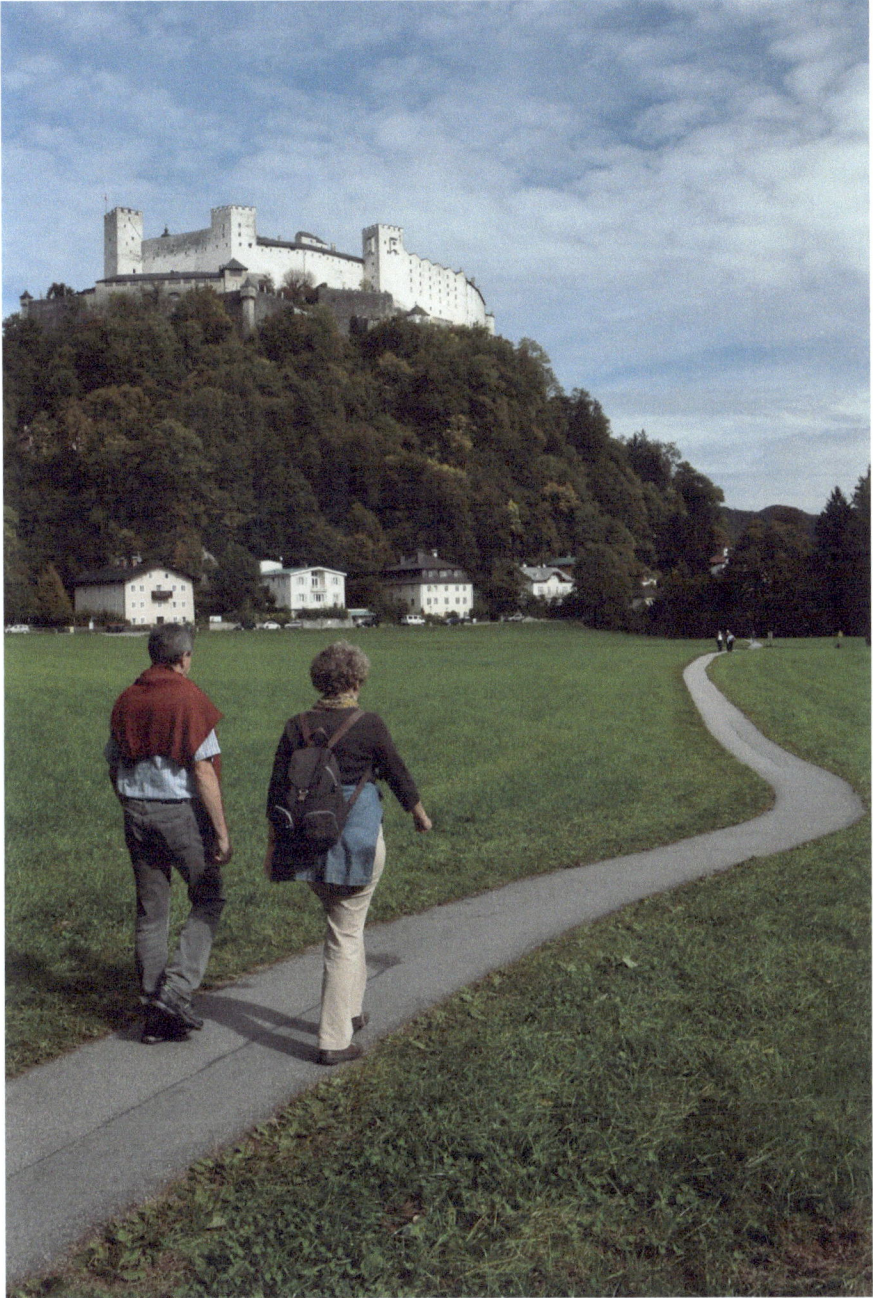

Figure 19-2: *Hohensalzburg Fortress looms over one of Salzburg's many protected landscapes.*

In the heart of Altstadt, Mozartplatz is a popular starting point for walking and bicycling itineraries. Heading west, hikers trek up the wooded paths of Monchsberg Mountain and contemplate the remnants of fortifications built in the 17th Century to defend Salzburg. Wandering north on Monchsberg, walkers arrive at Schloss Monchstein, a 14th-Century castle that has since morphed into a five-star hotel. The southward paths of Monchsberg lead to the Hohensalzburg Fortress, built in 1077 and today the largest, totally-preserved fortress in Central Europe (Salzburg, 2015).

East of Altstadt, Kuputzinerberg Mountain offers habitat to deer, badgers, martens and chamois, a species of goat-antelope native to the European mountains. A footpath here passes religious dioramas from the 18th Century, a 16th-Century monastery and 17th-Century fortifications built to protect Salzburg during the 30-Years War. At the summit, hikers can revive at Das Franziskischlossl, a restaurant housed in a small castle built in 1529 (Franziskischloessl, 2015).

Figure 19-3: *Separate bike and pedestrian paths line the banks of the Salzach River.*

Mirabell Gardens completes the greenbelt north of Altstadt. The gardens surround the Mirabell Palace, which houses the Marble Hall, formerly the prince-archbishop's ballroom and a concert venue for the Mozart family. The gardens themselves date from 1690 and today form a green link between Kapuzinerberg Mountain and Monchsberg Mountain using the Mullner Steg footbridge over the Salzach River.

The tree-lined riverbanks add a linear greenway to central Salzburg with bicycle/foot paths that traverse the entire UNESCO site. The bikeways here are part of Salzburg's 170-km cycle path network. In turn, these bikeways connect with regional bike routes like the 450-km Mozart Bike Path, which starts in Mozartplatz and meanders for 450-km through the lake district of Salzburg and Bavaria (Salzburg, 2015).

While preserving the Altstadt, Salzburg has been redeveloping some of its declining neighborhoods using advanced conservation and alternative energy concepts. In the Lehen district, the demolition of a soccer stadium triggered the transformation of an area of abandoned stores and neglected buildings. As one of 58 pilot projects cities in the European Union's CONCERTO program, Salzburg and its partners reduced energy demand by 70 percent through the refurbishment of 12 existing structures. In the 13 new buildings constructed within the CONCERTO framework, energy demand is 44 percent less than national averages. Residents were fully involved in the planning process which also led to the addition of new neighborhood facilities including a public library and elderly daycare center. As a demonstration of cutting edge sustainability features, Stadwerk Lehen features a thermal solar energy plant with a 2,000 square meter collector and a 200,000-liter tank for storing thermal energy which is connected to a local district heating system (Bahr, 2014).

Over time, Salzburg plans to transform its sparsely-developed areas into urban neighborhoods that are served by greenspace and built at higher densities using renewable energy and, ideally, connected to the city's district heating network. This infill model aims to accommodate a growing population while minimizing sprawl into the surrounding countryside, thereby protecting an alpine landscape that warrants preservation to the same extent as Salzburg's historic center (European Green Cities, 2015).

CHAPTER 20

Heidelberg, Germany: Higher degrees of sustainability

Heidelberg is famous for its prestigious university, historic monuments and cultural achievements. But this city of 150,000 people in south-western Germany also won the European Sustainable City Award twice from the European Commission and received the 2015 Global Green City Award from the Global Forum on Human Settlements and United Nations Environmental Program as well as prizes for urban redevelopment, bicycle-friendliness, transportation innovation, climate protection, energy conservation and preservation of the natural environment (Heidelberg, 2016).

Heidelberg is literally green. Of its total land area, only 29 percent is urbanized, while 27 percent is farmed and an impressive 41 percent is forested (Graczyk, 2015). The historic city center hugs both banks of the Neckar River with the Odenwald Mountains and the Heidelberg Castle forming the City's southern backdrop while the woods of Heiligenberg Mountain rise above Heidelberg University on the northern riverbank. To preserve this iconic setting, the City adopted an Old Heidelberg protective statute in 1997 that preserves the surrounding hills as well as the Castle and Old Town (Heidelberg, 2007).

Figure 20-1: *Heidelberg preserves its greenbelt, waterways and historic character including the 18th Century Old Bridge, now a pedestrian/cycle link over the Neckar River.*

To retain its green surroundings and provide efficient infrastructure, Heidelberg concentrates growth in areas near the city center and along public transportation routes. The City promotes infill growth, including the redevelopment of vacant or underutilized industrial land (Heidelberg, 2007). Most notably, Heidelberg transformed a former railroad freight yard into the Bahnstadt District, a new-town-in-town mixing residential units with office space, schools, a private university, movie theaters, kindergartens and retail stores as well as a building called Sky Labs which serves as a center for science and technology. In addition to putting residents next to their daily needs, Bahnstadt saves energy by requiring all buildings to meet extremely low "passive house" efficiency standards (Lisella, 2014). With an area of 116 hectares, Bahnstadt is the world's largest passive house district (Passive House Institute, 2014).

Heidelberg aims to slash energy consumption in existing and well as new buildings. In 2000, Heidelberg's Mayor for Environment and Energy initiated formation of the regional Energy Efficiency Agency with the goal of saving 6 million kWh annually by retrofitting three percent of the region's older buildings every year. Beyond the benefits to energy consumption and CO_2 emissions, this project aims to create 1,100 jobs and inject $110 million euros of direct investment into the local economy (ICLEI, 2007).

Figure 20-2: *Bahnstadt is the world's largest passive house district.*

Heidelberg takes a highly creative approach to conserving energy in its own public buildings, allowing private energy retrofit companies to keep up to 80 percent of the savings generated by energy conservation projects. Residential units built on city-owned land must meet strict annual energy conservation targets of 65 kWh per square meter for single family homes and 50 kWh per square meter for units in multiple family structures (Beatley, 2000).

Since 2001, 25 percent of the energy supplied to Heidelberg's city-owned properties has come from alternative energy sources. This amounts to 7 million kWh per year, making Heidelberg probably Germany's largest buyer of green electricity. The extra cost of this

Figure 20-3: *Heidelberg's pedestrianized Hauptstrasse is considered one of the world's greatest streets.*

alternative energy represents additional revenue for the City's power supplier, which invests this money in alternative-energy improvements including photovoltaic systems on schools and a biogas heat/power plant at the zoo fueled by animal waste (Herrmann, 2002).

Heidelberg's transportation policy rests on a goal of building a City of Short Distances. Mobility is greatly improved if homes, jobs, schools, recreation, shopping and other everyday needs are close together. Additionally, as called for in the City's 2015 Land Use Plan, proximity allows streets to be transformed into "living space" (Heidelberg, 2007). To prove that this ideal is achievable as well as desirable, Heidelberg can point to its own Old Town, where most streets are reserved for pedestrians. In particular, Hauptstrasse, Old Town's mile-long, pedestrianized "main street" has been ranked with other world-class "great streets" like Barcelona's La Rambla for its human scale, architectural richness and diversity of uses (Beatley, 2000).

Heidelberg was an early adopter of traffic calming techniques as a way of increasing safety, encouraging non-motorized mobility and reducing CO2 emissions. The Kirchheim neighborhood showcases increased infrastructure for pedestrians, bicyclists and trams in conjunction with reduced roadway space for private automobiles. Some roads in Heidelberg limit traffic to seven km/h (or slightly more than four miles per hour), forcing motorists to slow down and respect walkers and bicyclists (James and Fereday, 1999). Traffic calming in Heidelberg has produced a 31 percent reduction in accidents and a 44 percent decline in casualties (Beatley, 2000).

In addition to awards for climate protection, ecomobility and sustainable redevelopment, the Heidelberg region's mammoth Geo-Naturepark Bergstrasse-Odenwald was included in the UNESCO Global Geopark network officially formed in November 2015 (EGN, 2016). Geo-Naturepark Bergstrasse-Odenwald extends between the Neckar, Main and Rhine rivers, encompassing 3,500 square kilometers of countryside as well as about 100 municipalities including the City of Heidelberg. Initially established in 1960 as one of Germany's first nature parks, Bergstrasse-Odenwald provides conservation of biodiversity, environmental education, sustainable tourism and a greenbelt that guards against potential sprawl while serving as a recreational venue literally at Heidelberg's front door.

From the Old Bridge over the Neckar River, hikers and mountain bikers can use the centuries-old Philosopher's Walk to climb the hill overlooking Old Town Heidelberg and wander around a 10,000-kilometer network of signposted trails (EGN, 2013).

REFERENCES

Chapter 1: Europe's Greenest Places

What are Ecocities?

Joss, Simon (Editor). 2012. *Tomorrow's Cities Today: Ecocity Indicators, Standards and Frameworks – Bellagio Conference Report. International Ecocities Initiative*. London: University of Westminster.

Joss, Simon. 2015. *Sustainable Cities: Governing for Urban Innovation.* London: Palgrave.

Moore, Jennie. 2015. Ecological Footprints and Lifestyle Archetypes: Exploring the Dimensions of Consumption and the Transformation Needed to Achieve Urban Sustainability. *Sustainability*. 2015, 7, 4747-4763. April 21, 2015.

Moore, Jennie, and Rees, William. Getting to One-Planet Living. Chapter 4 in *State of the World 2013: Is Sustainability Still Possible?* New York: The Worldwatch Institute.

Green Structure

Akerlund, Ulrika. 2011. *Stockholm's Green Wedges – Concepts, learning and collaboration on urban and peri-urban forestry.* Stockholm: Boverket – Swedish National Board of Housing, Buildings and Planning.

Copenhagen. 2011. *Application for European Green Capital 2014.* Copenhagen: City of Copenhagen.

EGC [European Green Capital]. 2015. *Expert Panel – Technical Assessment Synopsis Report. European Green Capital Award 2017.* Brussels: European Commission.

Environmental Studies Centre. 2012. *The Interior Green Belt: Towards an Urban Green Infrastructure in Vitoria-Gasteiz.* Vitoria-Gasteiz: Environmental Studies Centre.

Essen. 2014. *Application – European Green Capital 2017.* Essen: City of Essen.

European Union. 2012. *Vitoria-Gasteiz – European Green Capital 2012.* Brussels: European Union.

European Commission. 2010. *Stockholm: European Green Capital 2010.* Brussels: European Commission.

European Commission. 2011. *Hamburg: European Green Capital 2011.* Brussels: European Commission.

European Commission. 2016. Nantes – Winner 2013 - European Green Capital. Retrieved on May 19, 2016 from http://ec.europa.eu/environment/europeangreencapital/wp-content/uploads/2011/04/Nantes-Leaflet-EN.pdf.

Floater, Graham, Rode, Phillip and Zenghelis, Dimitri. 2013. *Stockholm: Green Economy Leader Report.* London: London School of Economics and Political Science.

Freiburg. 2008. Freiburg Green City: Approaches to Sustainability. Freiburg: City of Freiburg im Breisgau.

Freiburg. 2011. *Environmental Policy in Freiburg.* Freiburg: City of Freiburg im Breisgau.

Hamburg. Undated. *GrunesNetzHamburg: The Landscape Programme Hamburg.* Hamburg: City of Hamburg.

Helsinki. 2013. *Helsinki City Plan – Vision 2050: Urban Plan –The New Helsinki City Plan.* Helsinki: City Planning Department.

Helsinki. 2015a. Undated web pages titled Central Park – Close to the Forest, Nature in the City. Retrieve on December 1, 2015 from

http://www.hel.fi/hel2/keskuspuisto/eng/1centralpark/.

Helsinki. 2015b. Undated paper titled Green Areas System in Helsinki. Helsinki: City Planning Department. Retrieved on December 1, 2015 from http://www.kirjavasatama.fi/pdf/southharbour_greenareassystem_helsinki.pdf.

Jaakkola, Maria. 2012. Helsinki, Finland: Greenness and Urban Form in Beatley, Timothy (ed). *Green Cities of Europe.* Washington D.C.: Island Press.

Jorgensen, Karsten and Kine, Thoren. 2012. 'Planning for a Green

Oslo' in Luccarelli, Mark and Roe, Per Gunnar, (eds), *Green Oslo: Visions, Planning and Discourse*. Farnham, Surrey, England: Ashgate Publishing.

Lantz, Gunnar. 2001. *Stockholm City Plan 1999: The City of Stockholm*. Stockholm: City of Stockholm.

Lekberg, Asa. 2010. Dense and Green: The Stockholm Region's Ten Wedges – as they will be preserved, improved and made more accessible. *The Region of Stockholm: Extracts from the Office of Regional Planning's Magazine*. Stockholm: Office of Regional Planning.

Munster. 2009. *The Munster Application for the European Green Capital Award*. Munster: City of Munster.

Munster. 2016. Cycle tours in and around Munster: Route of 100 Castles. Retrieved on 2-29-16 from http://www.muenster.de/stadt/tourismus/en/bicycle-tours_100-castles.html.

Nantes. 2010. *Application: European Green Capital Award Nantes 2012 – 2013*.

Nantes: Nantes Metropole.

Nelson, Alyse. *Stockholm, Sweden – City of Water*. Undated. Retrieved on May 22, 2016 from http://depts.washington.edu/open2100/Resources/1_OpenSpaceSystems/Open_Space_Systems/Stockholm_Case_Study.pdf.

Office of Regional Planning. 2010. *RUFS 2010* [Regional Development Plan Stockholm]. Stockholm: Office of Regional Planning.

O'Neill, Katie & Rudden, PJ. 2010. *Environmental Best Practice &*

Benchmarking Report: European Green Capital Award 2012 and 2013. Brussels: European Commission.

Valentine, Mark (translation). 2010. The Path of Remembrance and Comradeship. Ljubljana: Ljubljana Tourism.

Vejre, Henrik, Petersen, Hans and Henchel, Katja. Undated. The Copenhagen 1948 Finger Plan – A Comprehensive Plan for Urban Growth, Infrastructure and Open Space. Power Point Program. Retrieved on June 5, 2016 from http://www.plurel.net/images/muri_vejre.pdf.

Vitoria-Gasteiz. 2010. Application – European Green Capital Award 2012-2013. Vitoria-Gasteiz: City of Vitoria Gasteiz.

Vitoria-Gasteiz. 2016. The Green Belt of Vitoria Gasteiz. Retrieved on June 28, 2016 from https://www.vitoria-gasteiz.org/we001/was/we001Action.do?idioma=en&aplicacion=wb021&tabla=contenido&uid=u_1e8934a8_12e47a4954c__7ffd.

Access by Proximity

Bristol. 2012. *European Green Capitals Application 2015*. Bristol: City of Bristol.

European Commission. 2010. *The Expert Panel's Evaluation Work & Final Recommendations for the European Green Capital Award of 2012 and 2013*. Brussels: European Commission.

European Union. 2012. *Vitoria-Gasteiz – European Green Capital 2012*. Brussels: European Union.

Floater, Graham, Rode, Phillip and Zenghelis, Dimitri. 2013. *Stockholm: Green Economy Leader Report*. London: London School of Economics and Political Science.

Freiburg. 2008. Freiburg Green City: Approaches to Sustainability. Freiburg: City of Freiburg im Breisgau.

Freiburg. 2011. *Environmental Policy in Freiburg*. Freiburg: City of Freiburg im Breisgau.

Oslo. 2009. *European Green Capital Application from Oslo Including Additional Information*. Oslo: City of Oslo.

Register, Richard. 1987. *Ecocity Berkeley: Building Cities for a Healthy Future*. Berkeley: North Atlantic Books.

Register, Richard. 2016. Driverless cars? Bad Idea. How about driverless cities? Essay scheduled for September 2016 issue of *Ecocities Emerging*, newsletter of Ecocity Builders: www.ecocitybuilders.org.

Vitoria-Gasteiz. 2010. Application – European Green Capital Award 2012-2013. Vitoria-Gasteiz: City of Vitoria Gasteiz.

Feet First

Beatley, Timothy. 2000. *Green Urbanism: Learning from European Cites*. Washington: Island Press.

Berrini, Maria and Bono, Lorenzo. 2010. *Measuring Urban Sustainability: Analysis of the European Green Capital Award 2010 & 2011 application round.* Brussels: European Commission.

European Commission. 2010. *The Expert Panel's Evaluation Work & Final Recommendations for the European Green Capital Award of 2012 and 2013.* Brussels: European Commission.

European Union. 2012. *Vitoria-Gasteiz – European Green Capital 2012.* Brussels: European Union.

Freiburg. 2011. *Environmental Policy in Freiburg.* Freiburg: City of Freiburg im Breisgau.

Gehl, Jan. 2010, *Cities for People.* Washington, D.C.: Island Press.

Heidelberg. 2007. *Heidelberg City Development Plan 2015.* Heidelberg: City of Heidelberg.

Iwamiya, Manami, and Yeh, Yingu. 2011. Barcelona Waterfront. Retrieved on February 24, 2016 from https://courses.washington.edu/gehlstud/gehl-studio/wp-content/themes/gehl-studio/downloads/Autumn2011/A11_BarcelonaWaterfront.pdf.

James, Norman and Fereday, Davina. 1999. *Changing Travel Behavior.* Lichfield, UK: Transport and Travel Research, Ltd.

Medearis, Dale and Daseking, Wulf. 2012. Freiburg, Germany: Germany's Eco-Capital. In *Green Cities of Europe.* Timothy Beatley ed. Washington: Island Press.

O'Neill, Katie and MacHugh, Ian. 2013. *Urban Environment Good*

Practice & Benchmarking Report – European Green Capital Award 2015. Brussels: European Commission.

Speck, Jeff. 2012. *Walkable City: How Downtown Can Save America, One Step at a Time.* New York: North Point Press.

Taylor, Adam. 2012. How The Olympic Games Changed Barcelona Forever. *Business Insider.* July, 26, 2012.

UNESCO. 2015a. Historic Centre of the City of Salzburg. Retrieved on December 7, 2015 from http://whc.unesco.org/en/list/784.

UNESCO. 2015b. UNESCO World Heritage property Historic Centre of the City of Salzburg 1996. Retrieved on December 8, 2015 from http://whc.unesco.org/en/documents/101163.

Vitoria-Gasteiz. 2010. Application – European Green Capital Award 2012-2013. Vitoria-Gasteiz: City of Vitoria Gasteiz.

Eco-mobility

Barcelona. 2013. Urban Mobility Plan 2013-2018. Retrieved on February 24 from http://ajuntament.barcelona.cat/ecologiaurbana/en/what-we-do-and-why/active-and-sustainable-mobility/urban-mobility-plan.

Barcelona Yellow. 2016. Bicing: Bicycle Borrowing in Barcelona. Retrieved on February 24 from http://www.barcelonayellow.com/bcn-transport/78-bicing-city-bikes.

Beatley, Timothy. 2000. *Green Urbanism: Learning from European Cites.* Washington: Island Press.

Berrini, Maria, and Bono, Lorenzo. 2010. *Measuring Urban Sustainability: Analysis of the European Green Capital Award 2010 & 2011 Application Round.* Brussels: European Commission.

Bicycle Dutch. 2015. The F325 Fast Cycle Route Arnhem – Nijmegen. Accessed 7/5/16 from http://bicycledutch.wordpress.com/2015/09/29/the-f325-fast-cycle-route-qrnhem-nijemegen.

Bicycle Dutch. 2016a. Nijmegen, Cycling City of the Netherlands? Accessed on 7/5/16 from http://bicycledutch.wordpress.com/2016/04/05/nijmegen-cycling-city-of-the-Netherlands/.

Bicycle Dutch. 2016b. And the winner is… Accessed on July 6, 2016 from   https://bicycledutch.wordpress.com/2016/05/19/and-the-winner-is/.

Bristol. 2012. *European Green Capitals Application 2015.* Bristol: City of Bristol.

Copenhagen. 2007. *Eco-Metropolis: Our Vision for Copenhagen 2025.* Copenhagen: City of Copenhagen.

Copenhagen. 2011. *Application for European Green Capital 2014.* Copenhagen: City of Copenhagen.

Copenhagen. 2013. *City of Cyclists - Copenhagen Bicycle Life.* Copenhagen: City of Copenhagen.

Copenhagen. 2015. *Copenhagen Climate Projects – Annual Report 2015.* Copenhagen: City of Copenhagen.

European Commission. 2010a. *Stockholm: European Green Capital 2010.* Brussels: European Commission.

European Commission. 2010b. *The Experts Panel's Evaluation Work & Final Recommendations for the European Green Capital Award of 2012 and 2013.* Brussels: European Commission.

European Commission. 2016a. *European Green Capital Award 2018 – Technical Assessment Synopsis Report.* Brussels: European Commission.

European Commission. 2016b. Nantes – Winner 2013 - European Green Capital. Retrieved on May 19, 2016 from

http://ec.europa.eu/environment/europeangreencapital/wp-content/uploads/2011/04/Nantes-Leaflet-EN.pdf.

European Union. 2012. *Vitoria-Gasteiz – European Green Capital 2012.* Brussels: European Union.

Floater, Graham, Rode, Phillip and Zenghelis, Dimitri. 2013. *Stockholm: Green Economy Leader Report.* London: London School of Economics and Political Science.

Freiburg. 2011. *Environmental Policy in Freiburg.* Freiburg: City of Freiburg im Breisgau.

Gehl, Jan. 2010, *Cities for People*. Washington, D.C.: Island Press.

Hamburg, 2008. *Application for European Green Capital Award 2010-2011*. Hamburg: City of Hamburg.

James, Norman and Fereday, Davina. 1999. *Changing Travel Behavior*. Lichfield, UK: Transport and Travel Research, Ltd.

Medearis, Dale and Daseking, Wulf. 2012. Freiburg, Germany: Germany's Eco-Capital. In *Green Cities of Europe*. Timothy Beatley ed. Washington: Island Press.

Munich. 2010. *Munich: International – Sustainable – United in Solidarity*. Munich: Munich Department of Labor and Economic Development.

Munich. 2016. Biking. Retrieved on February 20, 2016 from http://www.muenchen.de/int/en/traffic/biking.html.

Munster. 2009. *The Munster Application for the European Green Capital Award*. Munster: City of Munster.

Munster. 2016. Cycling Capital. Retrieved on March 2, 2016 from http://www.muenster.de/en/cycling_capital.php.

Nantes. 2010. *Application: European Green Capital Award Nantes 2012 – 2013*.

Nantes: Nantes Metropole.

Nantes. 2014. *A review of 2013, Nantes European Green Capital*. Nantes: Nantes Metropole.

Nijmegen. 2015. *Application – European Green Capital 2018*. Nijmegen: City of Nijmegen.

Richelsen, Anders, and Sohuus, Martin, Eds. 2010. *Catalogue of Best Practice – Urban Sustainability – Learning from the Best: European Green Capital Award 2010 & 2011*. Brussels: European Commission.

Stockholm. 2008. *Application for European Green Capital Award.* Stockholm: City of Stockholm.

Sustrans, 2016. Vision to Reality in Bristol. Retrieved on 3-11-16 from http://www.sustrans.org.uk/about-us/vision-reality-bristol.

UCI [Union Cicliste Internationale]. 2014. Copenhagen, the most bicycle-friendly city in the world. Retrieved on June 7, 2016 from http://www.uci.ch/cyclingforall/copenhagen-the-most-bicycle-friendly-city-the-world/.

Union Cycliste Internationale. 2014. Hamburg: high on Europe's list of bike-friendly cities. Retrieved on June 2, 2016 from http://www.uci.ch/cyclingforall/hamburg-high-europe-list-bike-friendly-cities/.

Vitoria-Gasteiz. 2010. Application – European Green Capital Award 2012-2013. Vitoria-Gasteiz: City of Vitoria-Gasteiz.

Biodiversity

Bristol. 2012. *European Green Capitals Application 2015*. Bristol: City of Bristol.

ClimateWire. 2012. How the Dutch Make "Room for the River" by Redesigning Cities. *Scientific American.* January 20, 2012.

Consorci de Gallecs. 2015. Consortium Gallegos. Retrieved on December 17, 2015 from http://www.espairuralgallecs.cat.

EGC [European Green Capital]. 2014. *Expert Panel – Technical Assessment Synopsis Report. European Green Capital Award 2016.* Brussels: European Commission.

EGC [European Green Capital]. 2015. *Expert Panel – Technical Assessment Synopsis Report. European Green Capital Award 2017.* Brussels: European Commission.

EGN [European Geoparks Network]. 2013. The Geo-Naturepark Berstrasse-Odenwald. Retrieved on March 20, 2016 from http://geopark.come-to-web.net/en/service/infomaterial.php and https://translate.googleusercontent.com/translate_c?depth=1&hl=en&prev=search&rurl=translate.google.com&sl=de&u=http://www.geo-naturpark.net/deutsch/wir-ueber-uns/was-ist-das.php&usg=ALkJrhhYvLYf-8kkCwAxNXWgoZtAS3xCWg.

EGN [European Geoparks Network]. 2016. UNESCO Global Geoparks: A New Milestone for the Growing Geoparks Network. *European Geoparks Network Magazine.* Issue 13. Retrieved on March 21, 2016 from

http://www.geopark-terravita.de/page/uploads/files/downloads/06_-_egn_magazine_13_-_2016.pdf.

Environmental Studies Centre. 2012. *The Interior Green Belt: Towards an Urban Green Infrastructure in Vitoria-Gasteiz.* Vitoria-Gasteiz:

Environmental Studies Centre.

Essen. 2014. *Application – European Green Capital 2017*. Essen: City of Essen.

European Commission. 2009. *The Expert Panel's Evaluation Work & Final Recommendations for the European Green Capital Award of 2010 and 2011*. Brussels: European Commission.

European Commission. 2009. *The Expert Panel's Evaluation Work & Final Recommendations for the European Green Capital Award of 2010 and 2011*. Brussels: European Commission.

European Commission. 2010. *Stockholm: European Green Capital 2010*. Brussels: European Commission.

European Commission. 2011. *Hamburg: European Green Capital 2011*. Brussels: European Commission.

European Commission. 2015. Project LIFE: Gallecs. Retrieved on December 18, 2015 from http://ec.europa.eu/environment/life/project/Projects/index.cfm?fuseaction=search.dspPage&n_proj_id=2094#RM.

European Union. 2012. *Vitoria-Gasteiz – European Green Capital 2012*. Brussels: European Union.

Freiburg. 2011. *Environmental Policy in Freiburg*. Freiburg: City of Freiburg im Breisgau.

Hamburg, 2008. *Application for European Green Capital Award 2010-2011*. Hamburg: City of Hamburg.

Hamburg. 2012. *Hamburg – European Green Capital 2011 Final Report.* Hamburg: City of Hamburg.

Hamburg Port Authority. 2013. *Greening the Gateway to the World: Sustainability* Report 2011 – 2012. Hamburg: Hamburg Port Authority.

HUD User. 2015. A Dutch Approach to Flood Resilience. Accessed on July 2, 2016 from https://www.huduser.gov/portal/periodicals/em/winter15/highlight3_sidebar.html.

Ljubljana. 2013. European Green Capital 2016 Application. Ljubljana: City of Ljubljana.

Medearis, Dale and Daseking, Wulf. 2012. Freiburg, Germany: Germany's Eco-Capital. In *Green Cities of Europe.* Timothy Beatley ed. Washington: Island Press.

Munich. 2010. *Munich: International – Sustainable – United in Solidarity.* Munich: Munich Department of Labor and Economic Development.

Nijmegen. 2015. *Application – European Green Capital 2018.* Nijmegen: City of Nijmegen.

O'Neill, Katie & Rudden, PJ. 2010. *Environmental Best Practices and Benchmarking Report: European Green Capital Award 2012 – 2013.* Brussels: European Commission.

Oppermann, Bettina. 2005. Redesign of the River Isar in Munich, Germany: Getting coherent quality for green structures through the competitive process design? Part of Chapter Three in *Green Structure and Urban Planning.* Brussels: European Commission – European Cooperation in the Field of Scientific & Technical Research (COST

Action C11).

Treanor, Angela, Connolly, Louise and McEvoy, Brenda. 2014. *Urban Environment Good Practice & Benchmarking Report – European Green Capital Award 2016*. Brussels: European Commission.

UNESCO. 2015. UNESCO World Heritage property Historic Centre of the City of Salzburg 1996. Retrieved on December 8, 2015 from http://whc.unesco.org/en/documents/101163.

Vitoria-Gasteiz. 2010. Application – European Green Capital Award 2012-2013. Vitoria-Gasteiz: City of Vitoria Gasteiz.

Vitoria-Gasteiz. 2016. The Green Belt of Vitoria Gasteiz. Retrieved on June 28, 2016 from https://www.vitoria-gasteiz.org/we001/was/we001Action.do?idioma=en&aplicacion=wb021&tabla=contenido&uid=u_1e8934a8_12e47a4954c__7ffd

Brownfields to Ecodistricts

Bahr, Valerie. Ed. 2014. *Energy Solutions for Smart Cities and Communities: Lessons learnt from the 58 pilot cities of the CONCERTO initiative*. Stuttgart: European Union.

Baumer, Doris. 2009. *Living in Car-Reduced and Car-Free Residential Areas: A Promising Approach to Create Livable Neighborhoods and to Foster the Choice of Sustainable Means of Transport*. Dortmund: ILS-Research Institute for Regional and Urban Development gGmbH.

Berrini, Maria and Bono, Lorenzo. 2010. *Measuring Urban*

Sustainability: Analysis of the European Green Capital Award 2010 & 2011 application round. Brussels: European Commission.

Bristol. 2012. *European Green Capitals Application 2015*. Bristol: City of Bristol.

Copenhagen. 2011. *Application for European Green Capital 2014*. Copenhagen: City of Copenhagen.

Copenhagen. 2012. *Copenhagen: Solutions for Sustainable Cities*. Copenhagen: City of Copenhagen.

Essen. 2014. *Application – European Green Capital 2017*. Essen: City of Essen.

Europaconcorsi. 2015. Hessenberg Urban Renewal. Retrieved on July 2, 2016 from https://divisare.com/projects/243485-awg-architecten-Hessenberg-Urban-Renewal.

European Commission. 2011. *Hamburg: European Green Capital 2011*. Brussels: European Commission.

European Commission. 2012. *Expert Evaluation Panel – Synopsis Technical Assessment Report – European Green Capital Award 2014*. Brussels: European Commission.

Floater, Graham, Rode, Phillip and Zenghelis, Dimitri. 2013. *Stockholm: Green Economy Leader Report*. London: London School of Economics and Political Science.

Franne, Lars. 2007. *Hammarby Sjostad – a unique environmental project in*

Stockholm. Stockholm: GlashusEtt.

Freiburg. 2011. *Environmental Policy in Freiburg*. Freiburg: City of Freiburg im Breisgau.

Gehl, Jan. 2010. *Cities for People*. Washington: Island Press.

Hamburg, 2008. *Application for European Green Capital Award 2010-2011*. Hamburg: City of Hamburg.

Heidelberg. 2007. *Heidelberg City Development Plan 2015*. Heidelberg: City of Heidelberg.

Helsinki. 2009. *Walking in Arabianranta*. Helsinki: City Planning Department.

Hure, Vincent. 2013. *Concerto – act2 project: action of cities to mainstream energy efficient building and renewable energy systems across Europe*. Nantes: European Commission.

Jaakkola, Maria. 2012. Helsinki, Finland: Greenness and Urban Form in Beatley, Timothy (ed). *Green Cities of Europe*. Washington D.C.: Island Press.

Jokinen, Heikki. 2015. National industrial icon Arabia ceramics factory to close down. *Trade Union News from Finland:* April 11, 2015. Retrieved on November 29, 2015 from http://www.heikkijokinen.info/en/trade-union-news-from-finland/887-national-industrial-icon-arabia-ceramics-factory-to-close-down.

Kreutz, Stefan. 2010. *Case Study Report – HafenCity, Hamburg*. Brussels: European Commission.

Lisella, Maria. 2014. Romantic Heidelberg;s Groundbreaking New Life as Germany's Silicon Valley. *German Life*. February/March 2014.

Medearis, Dale and Daseking, Wulf. 2012. Freiburg, Germany: Germany's Eco-Capital. In *Green Cities of Europe*. Timothy Beatley ed. Washington: Island Press.

Munich. 2004. *Assessment of Messestadt Riem: Sustainable urban development in Munich*. Munich: Landeshauptstadt Munich.

Munster. 2016. Car-free Residence – Gartensiedlung Weissenburg. Retrieved on 2-29-16 from http://www.muenster.de/stadt/exwost/practice_I1.html.

Nantes. 2010. *Application: European Green Capital Award Nantes 2012 – 2013*.

Nantes: Nantes Metropole.

Nijmegen. 2015. *Application – European Green Capital 2018*. Nijmegen: City of Nijmegen.

OECD [Office of Economic Cooperation and Development]: 2013. Green Growth in Stockholm, Sweden. Paris: OECD.

Oslo. 2009. *European Green Capital Application from Oslo Including Additional Information*. Oslo: City of Oslo.

Passive House Institute. 2014. Award for Heidelberg Passive House district now visible in the cityscape. Retrieved on March 19, 2016 from http://passivehouse-international.org/upload/2014_06_30_Bahnstadt-Heidelberg_Press_Release.pdf.

Richelsen, Anders, and Sohuus, Martin, Eds. 2010. *Catalogue of Best Practice – Urban Sustainability – Learning from the Best: European Green Capital Award 2010 & 2011.* Brussels: European Commission.

Stockholm. 2015. Stockholm – The First European Green Capital [Five-Year report]: Stockholm: City of Stockholm.

URBED/TEN Group. 2011. *Learning from Helsinki and Stockholm.* London: URBED [Urban and Economic Development, Ltd].

Climate Action and Alternative Energy

Berrini, Maria, and Bono, Lorenzo. 2010. *Measuring Urban Sustainability: Analysis of the European Green Capital Award 2010 & 2011 Application Round.* Brussels: European Commission.

Bristol. 2012. *European Green Capitals Application 2015.* Bristol: City of Bristol.

Copenhagen. 2011. *Application for European Green Capital 2014.* Copenhagen: City of Copenhagen.

Copenhagen. 2015. *Copenhagen Climate Projects – Annual Report 2015.* Copenhagen: City of Copenhagen.

Dezeen. 2014. Abandoned concrete bunker converted into a green power plant by IBA Hamburg. Retrieved on June 2, 2016 from http://www.dezeen.com/2014/02/14/abandoned-concrete-bunker-converted-into-a-green-power-plant-by-iba-hamburg/.

EGC [European Green Capital]. 2014. *Expert Panel – Technical*

Assessment Synopsis Report. European Green Capital Award 2016. Brussels: European Commission.

EGC [European Green Capital]. 2015. *Expert Panel – Technical Assessment Synopsis Report. European Green Capital Award 2017.* Brussels: European Commission.

Essen. 2014. *Application – European Green Capital 2017.* Essen: City of Essen.

European Commission. 2009. *The Expert Panel's Evaluation Work & Final Recommendations for the European Green Capital Award of 2010 and 2011.* Brussels: European Commission.

European Commission. 2010. *Stockholm: European Green Capital 2010.* Brussels: European Commission.

European Commission. 2011. *Hamburg: European Green Capital 2011.* Brussels: European Commission.

European Commission.2012. *Expert Evaluation Panel – Synopsis Technical Assessment Report – European Green Capital Award 2014.* Brussels: European Commission.

European Commission. 2014. *Sharing Copenhagen – Copenhagen European Green Capital 2014: A Review.* Brussels: European Commission.

European Commission. 2016. *European Green Capital Award 2018 – Technical Assessment Synopsis Report.* Brussels: European Commission.

Floater, Graham, Rode, Phillip and Zenghelis, Dimitri. 2013.

Stockholm: Green Economy Leader Report. London: London School of Economics and Political Science.

Franne, Lars. 2007. *Hammarby Sjostad – a unique environmental project in Stockholm*. Stockholm: GlashusEtt.

Freiburg. 2011. *Environmental Policy in Freiburg*. Freiburg: City of Freiburg im Breisgau.

Hamburg, 2008. *Application for European Green Capital Award 2010-2011*. Hamburg: City of Hamburg.

Hamburg. 2012. *Hamburg – European Green Capital 2011 Final Report*. Hamburg: City of Hamburg.

Hamburg. 2015. GALAB Laboratories is Hamburg's 1000th Partner of the Environment. Retrieved on June 2, 2016 from http://www.hamburg-news.hamburg/en/cluster/renewable-energy/galab-laboratories-1000th-partner-environment/

Hamburg. 2016. Four Renewable Energy Projects from Hamburg. Retrieved on May 31, 2016 from http://www.hamburg-news.hamburg/en/cluster/renewable-energy/four-renewable-energy-projects-hamburg/.

Herrmann, Silva. 2002. Awarded Projects within Climate Star 2002. Frankfurt: Climate Alliance. Retrieved on March 20, 2016 from http://www.klimabuendnis.org/fileadmin/inhalte/dokumente/ClimateStar2002_awardedProjects_en_01.pdf.

ICLEI [International Council for Local Environmental Initiatives]. 2007. Energy Efficiency through Environmental Management in Heidelberg, Germany [Nomination for World Clean Energy Award].

Retrieved on March 20, 2016 from http://www.cleanenergyawards.com/top-navigation/nominees-projects/nominee-detail/project/25/?cHash=d75a11ace5.

Mattauch, Melanie. 2015. Munster: The first German city to go fossil free. Fossil Free Europe. November 4, 2015. Retrieved on March 3, 2016 from

http://gofossilfree.org/europe/munster-the-first-german-city-to-go-fossil-free/.

Nijmegen. 2015. *Application – European Green Capital 2018*. Nijmegen: City of Nijmegen.

O'Neill, Katie and Rudden, PJ. 2012. *Good Practice Report: European Green Capital Award 2014*. Brussels: European Commission.

Oslo. 2008. *European Green Capital Application from Oslo Including Additional Information*. Oslo: City of Oslo.

O'Toole, Ashley, McEvoy, Brenda and Campion, Louise. 2015. *Urban Environment Good Practice & Benchmarking Report: European Green Capital Award 2017*. Brussels: European Commission.

Stockholm. 2008. *Application for European Green Capital Award*. Stockholm: City of Stockholm.

Stockholm. 2015. Stockholm – The First European Green Capital [Five-Year report]: Stockholm: City of Stockholm.

Torres Vedras. 2014. *European Green Leaf Application*. Torres Vedras:

Torres Vedras.

United Kingdom. 2009. The Code for Sustainable Homes: Case Studies. London: UK Department for Communities and Local Government.

Public Engagement

Bahr, Valerie. Ed. 2014. *Energy Solutions for Smart Cities and Communities: Lessons learnt from the 58 pilot cities of the CONCERTO initiative*. Stuttgart: European Union.

Consorci de Gallecs. 2015. Consortium Gallegos. Retrieved on December 17, 2015 from http://www.espairuralgallecs.cat.

EGC [European Green Capital] 2015. Green Cities Fit for Life: 2017 – Essen. Retrieved on March 24, 2016 from http://ec.europa.eu/environment/europeangreencapital/winning-cities/2017-essen/index.html.

European Commission. 2016. Nantes – Winner 2013 - European Green Capital. Retrieved on May 19, 2016 from

http://ec.europa.eu/environment/europeangreencapital/wp-content/uploads/2011/04/Nantes-Leaflet-EN.pdf.

Freiburg. 2011. *Environmental Policy in Freiburg*. Freiburg: City of Freiburg im Breisgau.

Helsinki. 2010. *Viikki Science Park and Latokartano Guide*. Helsinki: City Planning Department.

Joss, Simon. 2011. *Eco-Cities: A Global Survey*. London: University of

Westchester.

Moore, Jennie. 2015. Ecological Footprints and Lifestyle Archetypes: Exploring the Dimensions of Consumption and the Transformation Needed to Achieve Urban Sustainability. *Sustainability.* 2015, 7, 4747-4763. April 21, 2015.

Nantes. 2010. *Application: European Green Capital Award Nantes 2012 – 2013.*

Nantes: Nantes Metropole.

Rinne, Heikki. 2009. Green Affordable Housing Development Case Eco-Viikki, Finland. Presentation by Project Manager, City of Helsinki, June 25, 2009, Washington, D.C. Retrieved on November 26, 2015 from http://www.upv.es/contenidos/CAMUNISO/info/U0511281.pdf.

Torres Vedras. 2014. *European Green Leaf Application.* Torres Vedras: Torres Vedras.

Green is Good

Copenhagen. 2011. *Application for European Green Capital 2014.* Copenhagen: City of Copenhagen.

Copenhagen. 2015. *Copenhagen Climate Projects – Annual Report 2015.* Copenhagen: City of Copenhagen.

European Commission. 2011. *Hamburg: European Green Capital 2011.* Brussels: European Commission.

Floater, Graham, Rode, Phillip and Zenghelis, Dimitri. 2013. *Stockholm: Green Economy Leader Report*. London: London School of Economics and Political Science.

Franne, Lars. 2007. *Hammarby Sjostad – a unique environmental project in Stockholm*. Stockholm: GlashusEtt.

Freiburg. 2011. *Environmental Policy in Freiburg*. Freiburg: City of Freiburg im Breisgau.

.

Hamburg. 2012. *Hamburg – European Green Capital 2011 Final Report*. Hamburg: City of Hamburg.

Ljubljana Tourism. 2016. Ljubljana Tourism Statistics. 20XX. Retrieved on April 15, 2016 from https://www.visitljubljana.com/en/b2b-press/statistical-data/ljubljana-tourism-statistics-from-2002-to-2012/ and https://www.visitljubljana.com/en/b2b-press/statistical-data/ljubljana-tourism-statistics-2014/.

Nantes. 2014. *A review of 2013, Nantes European Green Capital*. Nantes: Nantes Metropole.

Portugal. 2015. *Tech Trail: Portugal West Region - Quality Coast*. Lisbon: Portugal Energy and Tourism.

Rohracher, Harald and Spath, Philipp. 2012. Transitions Toward Sustainability – Learning from Graz and Freiburg? *Serbian Architectural Journal*. 2012; 4(1) 75-98.

Sawday, Alistair. 2012. What makes Bristol the UK's green capital? The Guardian. Retrieved on March 15, 2016 from http://www.theguardian.com/sustainable-business/bristol-uk-

green-capital.

Chapter 2: Stockholm, Sweden – Build the city inwards

Akerlund, Ulrika. 2011. *Stockholm's Green Wedges – Concepts, learning and collaboration on urban and peri-urban forestry*. Stockholm: Boverket – Swedish National Board of Housing, Buildings and Planning.

Berrini, Maria, and Bono, Lorenzo. 2010. *Measuring Urban Sustainability: Analysis of the European Green Capital Award 2010 & 2011 Application Round*. Brussels: European Commission.

European Commission. 2010. *Stockholm: European Green Capital 2010*. Brussels: European Commission.

Floater, Graham, Rode, Phillip and Zenghelis, Dimitri. 2013. *Stockholm: Green Economy Leader Report*. London: London School of Economics and Political Science.

Franne, Lars. 2007. *Hammarby Sjostad – a unique environmental project in Stockholm*. Stockholm: GlashusEtt.

Lantz, Gunnar. 2001. *Stockholm City Plan 1999: The City of Stockholm*. Stockholm: City of Stockholm.

Lekberg, Asa. 2010. Dense and Green: The Stockholm Region's Ten Wedges – as they will be preserved, improved and made more accessible. *The Region of Stockholm: Extracts from the Office of Regional Planning's Magazine*. Stockholm: Office of Regional Planning.

Nelson, Alyse. *Stockholm, Sweden – City of Water*. Undated. Retrieved on May 22, 2016 from http://depts.washington.edu/open2100/Resources/1_OpenSpaceSystems/Open_Space_Systems/Stockholm_Case_Study.pdf.

OECD [Office of Economic Cooperation and Development]: 2013. Green Growth in Stockholm, Sweden. Paris: OECD.

Office of Regional Planning. 2010. *RUFS 2010* [Regional Development Plan Stockholm]. Stockholm: Office of Regional Planning.

Richelsen, Anders, and Sohuus, Martin, Eds. 2010. *Catalogue of Best Practice – Urban Sustainability – Learning from the Best: European Green Capital Award 2010 & 2011*. Brussels: European Commission.

Stockholm. 2008. *Application for European Green Capital Award*. Stockholm: City of Stockholm.

Stockholm. 2015. Stockholm – The First European Green Capital [Five-Year report]: Stockholm: City of Stockholm.

Stockholm. 2016. Stockholm Royal Seaport. Retrieved on May 21, 2016 from http://international.stockholm.se/globalassets/ovriga-bilder-och-filer/visionsrs2030_medium.pdf.

URBED/TEN Group. 2011. *Learning from Helsinki and Stockholm*. London: URBED [Urban and Economic Development, Ltd].

Chapter 3: Hamburg, Germany: The business of sustainability

Berrini, Maria, and Bono, Lorenzo. 2010. *Measuring Urban Sustainability: Analysis of the European Green Capital Award 2010 & 2011 Application Round.* Brussels: European Commission.

Dezeen. 2014. Abandoned concrete bunker converted into a green power plant by IBA Hamburg. Retrieved on June 2, 2016 from http://www.dezeen.com/2014/02/14/abandoned-concrete-bunker-converted-into-a-green-power-plant-by-iba-hamburg/.

European Commission. 2009. *The Expert Panel's Evaluation Work & Final Recommendations for the European Green Capital Award of 2010 and 2011.* Brussels: European Commission.

.

European Commission. 2011. *Hamburg: European Green Capital 2011.* Brussels: European Commission.

Hamburg, 2008. *Application for European Green Capital Award 2010-2011.* Hamburg: City of Hamburg.

Hamburg. 2012. *Hamburg – European Green Capital 2011 Final Report.* Hamburg: City of Hamburg.

Hamburg. 2015. GALAB Laboratories is Hamburg's 1000th Partner of the Environment. Retrieved on June 2, 2016 from http://www.hamburg-news.hamburg/en/cluster/renewable-energy/galab-laboratories-1000th-partner-environment/

Hamburg. 2016. Four Renewable Energy Projects from Hamburg. Retrieved on May 31, 2016 from http://www.hamburg-news.hamburg/en/cluster/renewable-energy/four-renewable-energy-projects-hamburg/.

Hamburg Port Authority. 2013. *Greening the Gateway to the World: Sustainability* Report 2011 – 2012. Hamburg: Hamburg Port Authority.

Hamburg. Undated. *GrunesNetzHamburg: The Landscape Programme Hamburg.* Hamburg: City of Hamburg.

Kreutz, Stefan. 2010. *Case Study Report – HafenCity, Hamburg.* Brussels: European Commission.

Union Cycliste Internationale. 2014. Hamburg: high on Europe's list of bike-friendly cities. Retrieved on June 2, 2016 from http://www.uci.ch/cyclingforall/hamburg-high-europe-list-bike-friendly-cities/.

Chapter 4: Vitoria-Gasteiz, Spain: Growing up – not out

Environmental Studies Centre. 2012. *The Interior Green Belt: Towards an Urban Green Infrastructure in Vitoria-Gasteiz.* Vitoria-Gasteiz: Environmental Studies Centre.

European Commission. 2010. *The Expert Panel's Evaluation Work & Final Recommendations for the European Green Capital Award of 2012 and 2013.* Brussels: European Commission.

European Union. 2012. *Vitoria-Gasteiz – European Green Capital 2012*. Brussels: European Union.

O'Neill, Katie & Rudden, PJ. 2010. *Environmental Best Practices and Benchmarking Report: European Green Capital Award 2012 – 2013*. Brussels: European Commission.

Vitoria-Gasteiz. 2010. Application – European Green Capital Award 2012-2013. Vitoria-Gasteiz: City of Vitoria Gasteiz.

Vitoria-Gasteiz. 2016. The Green Belt of Vitoria Gasteiz. Retrieved on June 28, 2016 from https://www.vitoria-gasteiz.org/we001/was/we001Action.do?idioma=en&aplicacion=wb021&tabla=contenido&uid=u_1e8934a8_12e47a4954c_7ffd

Chapter 5: Nantes, France: City of eco-neighborhoods

European Commission. 2010. *The Experts Panel's Evaluation Work & Final Recommendations for the European Green Capital Award of 2012 and 2013*. Brussels: European Commission.

European Commission. 2016. Nantes – Winner 2013 - European Green Capital. Retrieved on May 19, 2016 from

http://ec.europa.eu/environment/europeangreencapital/wp-content/uploads/2011/04/Nantes-Leaflet-EN.pdf.

Hure, Vincent. 2013. *Concerto – act2 project: action of cities to mainstream energy efficient building and renewable energy systems across Europe.* Nantes: European Commission.

Nantes. 2010. *Application: European Green Capital Award Nantes 2012 – 2013.*

Nantes: Nantes Metropole.

Nantes. 2014. *A review of 2013, Nantes European Green Capital.* Nantes: Nantes Metropole.

O'Neill, Katie & Rudden, PJ. 2010. *Environmental Best Practice & Benchmarking Report: European Green Capital Award 2012 and 2013.* Brussels: European Commission.

Chapter 6: Copenhagen, Denmark: Good cycle karma

Copenhagen. 2007. *Eco-Metropolis: Our Vision for Copenhagen 2025.* Copenhagen: City of Copenhagen.

Copenhagen. 2011. *Application for European Green Capital 2014.* Copenhagen: City of Copenhagen.

Copenhagen. 2012. *Copenhagen: Solutions for Sustainable Cities.* Copenhagen: City of Copenhagen.

Copenhagen. 2013. *City of Cyclists - Copenhagen Bicycle Life.* Copenhagen: City of Copenhagen.

Copenhagen. 2015. *Copenhagen Climate Projects – Annual Report 2015*. Copenhagen: City of Copenhagen.

European Commission. 2012a. *Jury Report for the European Green Capital Award 2014*. Brussels: European Commission.

European Commission.2012b. *Expert Evaluation Panel – Synopsis Technical Assessment Report – European Green Capital Award 2014*. Brussels: European Commission.

European Commission. 2014. *Sharing Copenhagen – Copenhagen European Green Capital 2014: A Review*. Brussels: European Commission.

Gehl, Jan. 2010, *Cities for People*. Washington, D.C.: Island Press.

O'Neill, Katie and Rudden, PJ. 2012. *Good Practice Report: European Green Capital Award 2014*. Brussels: European Commission.

UCI [Union Cicliste Internationale]. 2014. Copenhagen, the most bicycle-friendly city in the world. Retrieved on June 7, 2016 from http://www.uci.ch/cyclingforall/copenhagen-the-most-bicycle-friendly-city-the-world/.

Vejre, Henrik, Petersen, Hans and Henchel, Katja. Undated. The Copenhagen 1948 Finger Plan – A Comprehensive Plan for Urban Growth, Infrastructure and Open Space. Power Point Program. Retrieved on June 5, 2016 from http://www.plurel.net/images/muri_vejre.pdf.

Chapter 7: Bristol, United Kingdom: Incubating change

Bristol. 2012. *European Green Capitals Application 2015*. Bristol: City of Bristol.

Bristol. 2013. UK's first Local Authority wind farm takes shape. Retrieved on March 15, 2016 from http://news.bristol.gov.uk/uks-first-local-authority-wind-farm-takes-shape.

European Commission. 2013. *Expert Panel – Synopsis Technical Assessment Report: European Green Capital Award 2015*. Brussels: European Commission.

Sawday, Alistair. 2012. What makes Bristol the UK's green capital? The Guardian. Retrieved on March 15, 2016 from http://www.theguardian.com/sustainable-business/bristol-uk-green-capital.

Sustrans, 2016. Vision to Reality in Bristol. Retrieved on 3-11-16 from http://www.sustrans.org.uk/about-us/vision-reality-bristol.

United Kingdom. 2009. The Code for Sustainable Homes: Case Studies. London: UK Department for Communities and Local Government.

Chapter 8: Ljubljana, Slovenia: River as centerpiece

Bordas, David. 2012. Preureditve nabrezij in mostovi na Ljubljanici. Retrieved on April 13, 2016 from http://www.publicspace.org/en/print-works/g072-preureditve-nabrezij-in-mostovi-na-ljubljanici.

EGC [European Green Capital]. 2014. *Expert Panel – Technical Assessment Synopsis Report. European Green Capital Award 2016.* Brussels: European Commission.

Ljubljana. 2013. European Green Capital 2016 Application. Ljubljana: City of Ljubljana.

Ljubljana Tourism. 2016. Ljubljana Tourism Statistics. 20XX. Retrieved on April 15, 2016 from https://www.visitljubljana.com/en/b2b-press/statistical-data/ljubljana-tourism-statistics-from-2002-to-2012/ and https://www.visitljubljana.com/en/b2b-press/statistical-data/ljubljana-tourism-statistics-2014/.

O'Neill, Katie and MacHugh, Ian. 2013. *Urban Environment Good Practice & Benchmarking Report – European Green Capital Award 2015.* Brussels: European Commission.

Treanor, Angela, Connolly, Louise and McEvoy, Brenda. 2014. *Urban Environment Good Practice & Benchmarking Report – European Green Capital Award 2016.* Brussels: European Commission.

Valentine, Mark (translation). 2010. The Path of Remembrance and Comradeship. Ljubljana: Ljubljana Tourism.

Chapter 9: Essen, Germany: Greening brownfields

EGC [European Green Capital] 2015a. *Jury Report – European Green Capital Award 2017*. Brussels: European Commission.

EGC [European Green Capital]. 2015b. *Expert Panel – Technical Assessment Synopsis Report. European Green Capital Award 2017*. Brussels: European Commission.

EGC [European Green Capital] 2015c. Green Cities Fit for Life: 2017 – Essen. Retrieved on March 24, 2016 from http://ec.europa.eu/environment/europeangreencapital/winni ng-cities/2017-essen/index.html.

Essen. 2014. *Application – European Green Capital 2017*. Essen: City of Essen.

O'Toole, Ashley, McEvoy, Brenda and Campion, Louise. 2015. *Urban Environment Good Practice & Benchmarking Report: European Green Capital Award 2017*. Brussels: European Commission.

Schulemann-Maier, Gaby. 2016. Bird sanctuary Heisinger Bow in Essen and Schellenberger forest with NSG leguminous trees in Essen. Retrieved on March 21, 2016 from http://www.fotoreiseberichte.de/.

Treanor, Angela, Connolly, Louise and McEvoy, Brenda. 2014. *Urban Environment Good Practice & Benchmarking Report – European Green Capital Award 2016*. Brussels: European Commission.

Chapter 10: Nijmegen, Netherlands: Room for the river

Bicycle Dutch. 2015. The F325 Fast Cycle Route Arnhem – Nijmegen. Accessed 7/5/16 from http://bicycledutch.wordpress.com/2015/09/29/the-f325-fast-cycle-route-qrnhem-nijemegen.

Bicycle Dutch. 2016a. Nijmegen, Cycling City of the Netherlands? Accessed on 7/5/16 from http://bicycledutch.wordpress.com/2016/04/05/nijmegen-cycling-city-of-the-Netherlands/.

Bicycle Dutch. 2016b. And the winner is… Accessed on July 6, 2016 from https://bicycledutch.wordpress.com/2016/05/19/and-the-winner-is/.

ClimateWire. 2012. How the Dutch Make "Room for the River" by Redesigning Cities. *Scientific American*. January 20, 2012.

Europaconcorsi. 2015. Hessenberg Urban Renewal. Retrieved on July 2, 2016 from https://divisare.com/projects/243485-awg-architecten-Hessenberg-Urban-Renewal.

European Commission. 2016. *European Green Capital Award 2018 – Technical Assessment Synopsis Report*. Brussels: European Commission.

Frehmann, T. and Althoff, A. 2010. Adapting urban water infrastructures to face the effects of climate change – from strategy to technical implementation. Accessed on July 6, 2016 from http://documents.irevues.inist.fr/bitstream/handle/2042/35653/11204-197FRE.pdf?s.

Future Cities. 2013. *The Future Cities Guide: Creating Livable and Climate-Proof Cities*. Essen: Lippeverband.

HUD User. 2015. A Dutch Approach to Flood Resilience. Accessed on July 2, 2016 from https://www.huduser.gov/portal/periodicals/em/winter15/highlight3_sidebar.html.

Nijmegen. 2007. *Groene Allure binnenstad Nijmegen*. Nijmegen: City of Nijmegen.

Nijmegen. 2015. *Application – European Green Capital 2018*. Nijmegen: City of Nijmegen.

Park Lingezegen. 2016. Park Lingezegen. Website at http://parklingezegen.nl/introductie-park-lingezegen/.

Chapter 11: Freiburg, Germany: Doing well by doing good

Berrini, Maria and Bono, Lorenzo. 2010. *Measuring Urban Sustainability: Analysis of the European Green Capital Award 2010 & 2011 application round*. Brussels: European Commission.

Freiburg. 2008. Freiburg Green City: Approaches to Sustainability. Freiburg: City of Freiburg im Breisgau.

Freiburg. 2011. *Environmental Policy in Freiburg*. Freiburg: City of Freiburg im Breisgau.

Medearis, Dale and Daseking, Wulf. 2012. Freiburg, Germany: Germany's Eco-Capital. In *Green Cities of Europe*. Timothy Beatley ed.

Washington: Island Press.

Rohracher, Harald and Spath, Philipp. 2012. Transitions Toward Sustainability – Learning from Graz and Freiburg? *Serbian Architectural Journal*. 2012; 4(1) 75-98.

Chapter 12: Torres Vedras, Portugal: Rediscovering wind power

European Commission. 2015. Expert Panel Technical Assessment Synopsis Report - European Green Leaf 2015 – May 2015. Retrieved on November 22, 2015 from http://www.EC.Europa.EU/Environment/EuropeanGreenCapital.

Moore, Jennie. 2015. Ecological Footprints and Lifestyles Archetypes: Exploring Dimensions of Consumption and the Transformation Needed to Achieve Urban Sustainability. *Sustainability*. April 21, 2015.

Portugal. 2015. *Tech Trail: Portugal West Region - Quality Coast*. Lisbon: Portugal Energy and Tourism.

Torres Vedras. 2014. *European Green Leaf Application*. Torres Vedras: Torres Vedras.

Chapter 13: Oslo, Norway: The blue and the green and the city in between

Beatley, Timothy. 2012. 'Biophilic Oslo' in Luccarelli, Mark and Roe, Per Gunnar, (eds), *Green Oslo: Visions, Planning and Discourse*. Farnham, Surrey, England: Ashgate Publishing.

European Commission. 2009. *The Expert Panel's Evaluation Work & Final Recommendations for the European Green Capital Award of 2010 and 2011*. Brussels: European Commission.

Gehl, Jan. 2010. *Cities for People*. Washington: Island Press.

Jorgensen, Karsten and Kine, Thoren. 2012. 'Planning for a Green Oslo' in Luccarelli, Mark and Roe, Per Gunnar, (eds), *Green Oslo: Visions, Planning and Discourse*. Farnham, Surrey, England: Ashgate Publishing.

Oslo. 2008. *European Green Capital Application from Oslo Including Additional Information*. Oslo: City of Oslo.

Chapter 14: Munster, Germany: City of short distances

Baumer, Doris. 2009. *Living in Car-Reduced and Car-Free Residential Areas: A Promising Approach to Create Livable Neighborhoods and to Foster the Choice of Sustainable Means of Transport*. Dortmund: ILS-Research Institute for Regional and Urban Development gGmbH.

Mattauch, Melanie. 2015. Munster: The first German city to go fossil free. Fossil Free Europe. November 4, 2015. Retrieved on March 3, 2016 from

http://gofossilfree.org/europe/munster-the-first-german-city-to-go-fossil-free/.

Munster. 2006. Improving the landscape: The Munster green space ordinance. Retrieved on 2-29-16 from http://www.muenster.de/stadt/livcom/index244.htm.

Munster. 2009. *The Munster Application for the European Green Capital Award.* Munster: City of Munster.

Munster. 2016a. Cycle tours in and around Munster: Route of 100 Castles. Retrieved on 2-29-16 from http://www.muenster.de/stadt/tourismus/en/bicycle-tours_100-castles.html.

Munster. 2016b. Cycling Capital. Retrieved on March 2, 2016 from http://www.muenster.de/en/cycling_capital.php.

Munster. 2016c. Car-free Residence – Gartensiedlung Weissenburg. Retrieved on 2-29-16 from http://www.muenster.de/stadt/exwost/practice_l1.html.

Chapter 15: Mollet del Valles, Spain: Agriculture as recreation

Consorci de Gallecs. 2015. Consortium Gallegos. Retrieved on December 17, 2015 from http://www.espairuralgallecs.cat.

European Commission. 2015a. Project LIFE: Gallecs. Retrieved on December 18, 2015 from http://ec.europa.eu/environment/life/project/Projects/index.cfm?fuseaction=search.dspPage&n_proj_id=2094#RM.

European Commission. 2015. Expert Panel Technical Assessment Synopsis Report - European Green Leaf 2015 – May 2015. Retrieved on November 22, 2015 from http://www.EC.Europa.EU/Environment/EuropeanGreenCapital.

MEET – Mediterranean Experience of Eco Tourism. 2014. Catalonia Region. Retrieved on December 15, 2015 from http://www.medecotourism.org/p5.asp.

Mollet del Valles. 2014. *European Green Leaf Application*. Mollet del Valles: Mollet del Valles.

URBACT. Diet for a Green Planet. Retrieved on December 15. 2015 from http://urbact.eu/diet-for-a-green-planet#.

Chapter 16: Helsinki, Finland: Planned for implementation

Arabia Story. Retrieved on November 29, 2015 from http://www.arabia.fi/en/Arabia-Story/History.

Helsinki. 2005. *Eco-Viikki: Aims, Implementation and Results*. Helsinki: City Ministry of the Environment.

Helsinki. 2009. *Walking in Arabianranta*. Helsinki: City Planning Department.

Helsinki. 2010. *Viikki Science Park and Latokartano Guide*. Helsinki: City Planning Department.

Helsinki. 2013. *Helsinki City Plan – Vision 2050: Urban Plan –The New Helsinki City Plan*. Helsinki: City Planning Department.

Helsinki. 2015a. Undated web pages titled Central Park – Close to the Forest, Nature in the City. Retrieve on December 1, 2015 from http://www.hel.fi/hel2/keskuspuisto/eng/1centralpark/.

Helsinki. 2015b. Undated paper titled Green Areas System in Helsinki. Helsinki: City Planning Department. Retrieved on December 1, 2015 from http://www.kirjavasatama.fi/pdf/southharbour_greenareassystem_helsinki.pdf.

Jaakkola, Maria. 2012. Helsinki, Finland: Greenness and Urban Form in Beatley, Timothy (ed). *Green Cities of Europe*. Washington D.C.: Island Press.

Jokinen, Heikki. 2015. National industrial icon Arabia ceramics factory to close down. *Trade Union News from Finland:* April 11, 2015. Retrieved on November 29, 2015 from http://www.heikkijokinen.info/en/trade-union-news-from-finland/887-national-industrial-icon-arabia-ceramics-factory-to-close-down.

Helsinki. *West Harbour: A long, luscious strip of seashore.* Helsinki: City Executive Office. Retrieved on December 1, 2015 from http://en.uuttahelsinkia.fi/sites/default/files/attachments/page-sections/lansisatama_eng_265x800_01122014_final.pdf

Joss, Simon. 2011.

Rinne, Heikki. 2009. Green Affordable Housing Development Case Eco-Viikki, Finland. Presentation by Project Manager, City of Helsinki, June 25, 2009, Washington, D.C. Retrieved on November 26, 2015 from http://www.upv.es/contenidos/CAMUNISO/info/U0511281.pdf.

URBED. 2011. *Learning from Helsinki and Stockholm*. London: URBED.

Chapter 17: Barcelona, Spain: Olympics as catalyst

Barcelona. 2012. *Citizen Commitment to Sustainability 2012 – 2022: For a More Equitable, Prosperous and Self-Sufficient Barcelona*. Barcelona: Barcelona City Council.

Barcelona. 2013a. Urban Mobility Plan 2013-2018. Retrieved on February 24 from http://ajuntament.barcelona.cat/ecologiaurbana/en/what-we-do-and-why/active-and-sustainable-mobility/urban-mobility-plan.

Barcelona 2013b. *Barcelona Green Infrastructure and Biodiversity Plan 2020*. Barcelona: Barcelona City Council.

Barcelona. 2015. Green spaces: the biodiversity at Montjuic. Retrieved on 9-4-15 from http://mediambient.itineraris.bcn.cat/en/node/684/364.

Barcelona. 2016. Green Corridors: Passeig de Sant Joan. Retrived on 2-25-16 from http://ajuntament.barcelona.cat/ecologiaurbana/en/what-we-do-and-why/green-city-and-biodiversity/green-corridors-passeig-de-sant-joan.

Barcelona Yellow. 2016. Bicing: Bicycle Borrowing in Barcelona. Retrieved on February 24 from http://www.barcelonayellow.com/bcn-transport/78-bicing-city-bikes.

Iwamiya, Manami, and Yeh, Yingu. 2011. Barcelona Waterfront. Retrieved on February 24, 2016 from https://courses.washington.edu/gehlstud/gehl-studio/wp-content/themes/gehl-studio/downloads/Autumn2011/A11_BarcelonaWaterfront.pdf.

Taylor, Adam. 2012. How The Olympic Games Changed Barcelona Forever. *Business Insider.* July, 26, 2012.

Chapter 18: Munich, Germany: Compact – urban – green

Munich. 2004. *Assessment of Messestadt Riem: Sustainable urban development in Munich.* Munich: Landeshauptstadt Munich.

Munich. 2005. *Shaping the Future of Munich.* Munich: Munich Department of Urban Planning and Building Regulation.

Munich. 2010. *Munich: International – Sustainable – United in Solidarity.* Munich: Munich Department of Labor and Economic Development.

Munich. 2016a. Englisher Garden. Retrieved on February 13, 2016 from

http://www.muenchen.de/int/en/sights/parks/english-garden.html.

Munich. 2016b. Biking. Retrieved on February 20, 2016 from http://www.muenchen.de/int/en/traffic/biking.html.

Oppermann, Bettina. 2005. Redesign of the River Isar in Munich, Germany: Getting coherent quality for green structures through the competitive process design? Part of Chapter Three in *Green Structure and Urban Planning*. Brussels: European Commission – European Cooperation in the Field of Scientific & Technical Research (COST Action C11).

Oppermann, Bettina and Pauleit, Stephan. 2005. The Greenstructure of Munich: The need for and risk of regional ccooperation. Part of Chapter Three in *Green Structure and Urban Planning*. Brussels: European Commission – European Cooperation in the Field of Scientific & Technical Research (COST Action C11).

Pauleit, Stephan. 2005. Munich. Part of Chapter Three in *Green Structure and Urban Planning*. Brussels: European Commission – European Cooperation in the Field of Scientific & Technical Research (COST Action C11).

Chapter 19: Salzburg, Austria: Walkability never gets old

Bahr, Valerie. Ed. 2014. *Energy Solutions for Smart Cities and Communities: Lessons learnt from the 58 pilot cities of the CONCERTO initiative*. Stuttgart: European Union.

European Green City. 2015. Salzburg Municipality, Austria. Retrieved

on December 8, 2015 from
http://europeangreencities.com/green-city-building/salzburg-municipality-austria.

Franziskischloessl. 2015. Das Franziskischlossl. Retrieved on December 8, 2015 from
http://www.franziskischloessl.at/schloessl.htm.

Salzburg. 2015. Salzburg.info. Retrieved on December 7, 2015 form
http://www.salzburg.info/en/.

UNESCO. 2015a. Historic Centre of the City of Salzburg. Retrieved on December 7, 2015 from http://whc.unesco.org/en/list/784.

UNESCO. 2015b. UNESCO World Heritage property Historic Centre of the City of Salzburg 1996. Retrieved on December 8, 2015 from http://whc.unesco.org/en/documents/101163.

Chapter 20: Heidelberg, Germany: Higher degrees of sustainability

Beatley, Timothy. 2000. *Green Urbanism: Learning from European Cites.* Washington: Island Press.

EGN [European Geoparks Network]. 2013. The Geo-Naturepark Berstrasse-Odenwald. Retrieved on March 20, 2016 from
http://geopark.come-to-web.net/en/service/infomaterial.php
and
https://translate.googleusercontent.com/translate_c?depth=1&hl=en&prev=search&rurl=translate.google.com&sl=de&u=h

ttp://www.geo-naturpark.net/deutsch/wir-ueber-uns/was-ist-das.php&usg=ALkJrhhYvLYf-8kkCwAxNXWgoZtAS3xCWg.

EGN [European Geoparks Network]. 2016. UNESCO Global Geoparks: A New Milestone for the Growing Geoparks Network. *European Geoparks Network Magazine*. Issue 13. Retrieved on March 21, 2016 from

http://www.geopark-terravita.de/page/uploads/files/downloads/06_-_egn_magazine_13_-_2016.pdf.

Graczyk, Alice. 2015. Implementation of Sustainable Development in the City of Heidelberg. *Acta Universitatis Lodziensis Folia Oeconomica*. 2 (313).

Heidelberg. 2002. *Heidelberg - Where Do We Stands, What Are Our Achievements? A First Report on the Implementation of the Heidelberg City Development Plan 2010*. Heidelberg: City of Heidelberg.

Heidelberg. 2007. *Heidelberg City Development Plan 2015*. Heidelberg: City of Heidelberg.

Heidelberg. 2016. Prizes and Awards Received by City of Heidelberg. Retrieved on March 16, 2016 from http://www.heidelberg.de/english,Len/Home/Live/Prizes+and+Awards.html.

Herrmann, Silva. 2002. Awarded Projects within Climate Star 2002. Frankfurt: Climate Alliance. Retrieved on March 20, 2016 from http://www.klimabuendnis.org/fileadmin/inhalte/dokumente/ClimateStar2002_awardedProjects_en_01.pdf.

ICLEI [International Council for Local Environmental Initiatives]. 2007. Energy Efficiency through Environmental Management in Heidelberg, Germany [Nomination for World Clean Energy Award]. Retrieved on March 20, 2016 from http://www.cleanenergyawards.com/top-navigation/nominees-projects/nominee-detail/project/25/?cHash=d75a11ace5.

James, Norman and Fereday, Davina. 1999. *Changing Travel Behavior.* Lichfield, UK: Transport and Travel Research, Ltd.

Lisella, Maria. 2014. Romantic Heidelberg;s Groundbreaking New Life as Germany's Silicon Valley. *German Life.* February/March 2014.

Passive House Institute. 2014. Award for Heidelberg Passive House district now visible in the cityscape. Retrieved on March 19, 2016 from http://passivehouse-international.org/upload/2014_06_30_Bahnstadt-Heidelberg_Press_Release.pdf.

ACKNOWLEDGEMENTS

As I mentioned in the Preface, this book resulted largely from my involvement with Ecocity Builders, where I currently serve as a member of the Board of Directors. This non-profit organization, dedicated to the emergence of cities in balance with nature, was founded by Richard Register, a pioneer of the sustainable cities movement. Richard's 1987 book, *Ecocity Berkeley: Building Cities for a Healthy Future* was a revelation to me. It advocated nothing less than a radical reshaping of our *existing* metropolitan areas into three-dimensional centers served by public transportation and surrounded by greenspace – the way the landscape looked before the ubiquitous automobile created the endless sprawl that characterizes most metropolitan regions of the United States today. At the time, I was a city planner struggling with bureaucracy while Richard was actually following the famous Daniel Burnham exhortation: "Make no little plans; they have no magic to stir men's blood." To this day, Richard continues to inform and inspire with countless presentations around the world and numerous publications including the seminal *Ecocities: Rebuilding Cities in Balance with Nature* and his most recent books: *World Rescue: An Economics Built on What We Build* and *Ecocities Illustrated: The Easily Built Visionary Future of Richard Register.*

Kirstin Miller, Executive Director and member of the Board of Directors, is guiding Ecocity Builders in exciting new directions. Urbinsight, our largest project at the moment, is a participatory mapping and planning process used in Cairo, Egypt, Casablanca, Morocco, Cusco, Peru and Medellin, Columbia to date. With Kirstin's oversight, a talented team of planner-programmers is now developing a platform that will enable Urbinsight to serve many more cities around the world.

Ecocity Builders President Steven Bercu ably leads a Board of Directors that, in addition to Kirstin and myself, includes Sahar Attia, Professor of Urban Planning and Design at Cairo University, Jeff Stein, President of the Cosanti Foundation, Costis Toregas, Associate Director of the GW Cyber Security Policy and Research Institute and Simon Joss, Professor of Science and Technology Studies, Director of the International Eco-City Initiative at the University of Westminster, United Kingdom, and also the author of *Sustainable Cities: Governing for Urban Innovation,* a comprehensive exploration of the history and current state of ecocities.

Ecocity Snapshots was greatly facilitated by the fact that the European Green Capitals competition is conducted in the English language and because I was able to benefit from the knowledge of the many experts who have judged the 126 applications submitted since that program's inception in 2008. However, the Ecocity Framework, another major project of Ecocity Builders, reminds me that the criteria used by the European Green Capitals program, while essential to this book, don't tell the whole story. In addition to the European Green Capitals indicators, the Ecocity Framework includes additional factors like culture, well-being, education, economy, governance and food systems plus an analysis of whether a city is living within the planet's carrying capacity or consuming more than its fair share of Earth's resources. Ecocity Builders is extremely fortunate to have the development of the Ecocity Framework sponsored by the British Columbia Institute of Technology (BCIT) and led by Jennie Moore, Associate Dean of BCIT's School of Construction and the Environment as well as Director of Sustainable Development and Environmental Stewardship. Jennie is the author of studies cited throughout this book including "Ecological Footprints and Lifestyle Archetypes: Exploring the Dimensions of Consumption and the Transformation Needed to Achieve Urban Sustainability" and (with William Rees) "Getting to One-Planet Living." As of August 2016, Jennie and a team of advisors continue to refine the Ecocity Framework indicators, including those needed to measure a city's progress toward one-planet living. As a sobering thought, although the poorer regions of Asia, Latin America and Africa contain one-planet cities, Europe is typically home to three-planet cities, meaning ones that would require three planets if everyone on Earth equaled their levels of consumption.

Finally, I want to acknowledge the European Commission itself. While the United States federal government continues to dither over climate change and many other challenges facing the planet, the European Commission has acted responsibly in various ways including the development and support of the European Green Capitals and European Green Leaf programs. Cities pursue sustainability for its inherent value including quality of life, economic prosperity, efficient public services, environmental justice and a recognition that we humans are not the only inhabitants on Earth. But the added motivation of competition has been known to encourage cities as well as individuals to pursue more ambitious goals than they otherwise might. Also, the European Commission uses these competitions as teachable moments, annually preparing a best-practices manual gleaned from the applications submitted each year. Furthermore, the expert panel reports are extensive, providing guidance on how applicants can improve their sustainability efforts regardless of whether or not they win.

Last but not least, many thanks to my wife Adrian for proof reading and for joining me on many of these excursions. And much appreciation also to Creative Juices for going the extra mile in the design and production of this book.

INDEX